The Faith
I Highly
Recommend

Also by John Thomas McLarty:

Stand at the Cross

To order, call **1-800-765-6955**.

Visit us at
www.reviewandherald.com
for information on other Review and Herald® products.

Adventist Spirituality* for Thinkers and Seekers

{ *The Faith I Highly Recommend }

John Thomas **McLarty**

REVIEW AND HERALD® PUBLISHING ASSOCIATION
Since 1861 | www.reviewandherald.com

Published by Review and Herald® Publishing Association, Hagerstown, MD 21741-1119

Review and Herald® titles may be purchased in bulk for educational, business, fund-raising, or sales promotional use. For information, e-mail SpecialMarkets@reviewandherald.com.

The Review and Herald® Publishing Association publishes biblically based materials for spiritual, physical, and mental growth and Christian discipleship.

The author assumes full responsibility for the accuracy of all facts and quotations as cited in this book.

Quotations from the Bible not otherwise credited are the author's own renderings—either from combining various English translations or from his own translation from the Greek.

Bible texts credited to Amplified are from *The Amplified Bible*, Old Testament copyright © 1965, 1987 by the Zondervan Corporation. *The Amplified New Testament* copyright © 1958, 1987 by the Lockman Foundation. Used by permission.

Scripture quotations identified CEV are from the Contemporary English Version. Copyright © American Bible Society 1991, 1995. Used by permission.

Bible texts credited to KJV are from the King James Version of the Bible.

Verses marked TLB are taken from *The Living Bible,* copyright © 1971 by Tyndale House Publishers, Wheaton, Ill. Used by permission.

Scriptures credited to NCV are quoted from *The Holy Bible, New Century Version,* copyright © 1987, 1988, 1991 by Word Publishing, Dallas, Texas 75039. Used by permission.

Texts credited to NEB are from *The New English Bible.* © The Delegates of the Oxford University Press and the Syndics of the Cambridge University Press 1961, 1970. Reprinted by permission.

Texts credited to NIV are from the *Holy Bible, New International Version.* Copyright © 1973, 1978, 1984, International Bible Society. Used by permission of Zondervan Bible Publishers.

Texts credited to NKJV are from the New King James Version. Copyright © 1979, 1980, 1982 by Thomas Nelson, Inc. Used by permission. All rights reserved.

Bible texts credited to TEV are from the *Good News Bible*—Old Testament: Copyright © American Bible Society 1976, 1992; New Testament: Copyright © American Bible Society 1966, 1971, 1976, 1992.

This book was
Edited by Raymond H. Woolsey
Copyedited by Kathy Pepper
Designed by Bryan Gray
Cover art © 2010 Thinkstock
Typeset: Bembo 11/13

PRINTED IN U.S.A.
15   14   13   12   11   5   4   3   2   1

Library of Congress Cataloging-in-Publication Data
McLarty, John, 1952-   .
   The faith I highly recommend : Adventist spirituality for thinkers and seekers / John Thomas McLarty.
      p. cm.
1. Church attendance. 2. Seventh-Day Adventists—Membership. I. Title.
   BX6154.M385 2011
   230'.6732—dc22
                              2010021802
ISBN 978-0-8280-2379-5

Contents

Introduction

When William first visited the Church of Advent Hope he identified himself as an agnostic. Before long, he moved from occasionally attending church with his wife on Saturday mornings to a whole-hearted embrace of Sabbath keeping. He was amazed to discover a community that took a whole day off every week for things such as conversation about God, art, philosophy, and theology. Most of the members of this church were young adults, in Manhattan to pursue their careers. Still, they enjoyed spending 24 hours every week shielded from the demands of work. Sabbath was like a park in time, a tranquil open space in the frenzy of the city. Inside this park, they savored an entire day devoted to cultivating relationships with people and God.

William reveled in it. He was a professor, but for one day a week he was free to be a learner instead of a teacher; an explorer, not a guide. He began Sabbathkeeping as a skeptic, but Sabbath provided a sanctuary where he could explore the world of faith without pressure. He became a believer. Nearly a decade later he formally joined the church.

Sabbath works. Especially given the pace of contemporary life, this park in time is a priceless aid in the cultivation of spiritual life.

Milton attended our church a few times and then asked to join. I refused. I told him we required members to participate in a small group (which was true). But the real reason I put him off was an inner reservation that I couldn't quite explain. In hindsight, I say the Holy Spirit prompted me. Although I said no to his joining our congregation, he and I talked frequently, and eventually he opened his heart.

Thirty years earlier, a minister had grievously wounded him by rejecting his nieces and nephews because of their race. Now those nieces and nephews were middle-aged. None of them participated in church life. Their lives were marred by drugs, crime, and dysfunctional relationships. All this misery seemed to flow directly from the actions of that preacher.

Milton was consumed with bitterness. His anger was understandable, but it was killing him. He needed to let it go, to forgive, so that he could move on in his life. But forgiving felt like condoning or at least minimizing the injustice he had witnessed. No one else was holding that minister

7

accountable. He was never punished or even reprimanded. Milton nursed his rage as his own personal answer to the monstrous evil he had witnessed.

Milton and I talked about the judgment. The Bible insists that God is watching and that He will balance the scales of justice. Milton grew assured that God had seen through the minister's facade of ecclesiastical status and professed piety. God, too, was angry. Milton slowly released this minister into God's hands, knowing that God would be a far more formidable guarantor of justice than Milton ever could be.

Milton never joined a small group. He did join our church—released from the ball and chain of rage, released by the doctrine of judgment into the joy of confident faith. For Milton, judgment was a priceless tool in the cultivation of spiritual life.

Our hunger for God, our conviction (or sometimes mere suspicion) that God exists and has a benevolent interest in us is not something we create. It is something we discover within ourselves. We can no more originate faith than we can put life in a seed. But just as we can cultivate the mysterious life in a seed, so, too, can we cultivate faith.

I grow cacti in my greenhouse. Some seeds sprout right away when I plant them. Other seeds have surprised me by coming up years after I planted them. I treat all the seeds in a particular batch the same. But they do not all respond the same way. Still, over the years I have learned certain approaches to the cultivation of cacti that are more helpful (and one or two practices that are counterproductive).

It is something like this in spiritual life. Its origin, like the germination of a seed, is mysterious. But in addition to the mystery of germination, there are principles of growth. The job of the church is to learn all we can about those principles and to help people incorporate them into their lives.

William and Milton, the people I mentioned above, are real people who found valuable help for their spiritual life in specific ideas or practices. In the course of preaching and listening to seekers and believers talk about God, I have come to prize a number of beliefs and practices that are highly effective in helping people move toward a more confident, effective spiritual life.

When I listen to people who are trying to make sense of God, their own lives, and the world, it seems to me that their first desire is to find ideas and practices that work. They are looking for concepts about God that connect with their deepest longings and convictions. Theories are helpful, but only as they connect with life as we actually live it. The beliefs and behaviors I describe in this book work. They help people cultivate a relationship with God.

In these pages I speak in my own voice, of course. What I write reflects my experience, my education, my thinking. But the spiritual treasures described here are not my own private discoveries. They are the result of 150 years of study, experience, debate, and divine leading within a particular community of believers—the Seventh-day Adventist Church. They are the treasures of my church, but they were never intended by God to be protected, sequestered away in some secure vault. God intended them for action, for sharing. God wants us to put them to work. I hope you will overlook my pride in showing them off.

I have great respect for scholarship. Quality scholarship is essential for the stability and health of the church. Attention to scholarship is essential for wise, balanced service as a pastor. But although I read scholarly books and admire my friends in academia, I am not a scholar. I am more like a theological artist. Using words, I endeavor to paint truthful pictures of God and of the best elements of my community. I do not pretend detachment or objectivity; rather, I offer the truth that comes from giving happy attention to one's beloved. I am unabashedly in love with my subject. In writing this book, I have collected and touched up field sketches made over three decades of observing and practicing our faith as a pastor.

May these word pictures do you good, is my prayer.

—John McLarty

{ God Is Love }

The First Adventist Conviction

God is love. Whoever lives in love lives in God, and God in him (1 John 4:16).

God is love. This is the most essential Adventist conviction. Other elements were strongly formative in the early years of the Adventist movement. Our self-understanding was strongly shaped by evangelistic lectures that focused on the authority of the Bible, the heavenly sanctuary, the Sabbath, and distinctive interpretations of the prophecies of Daniel and Revelation. However, these beliefs are not ends in themselves. I regard them as scaffolding that God used to support the community while we built a clearer understanding of His love. "God is love" is both the foundation and the goal of Adventist theology.

The most influential theological voice in Adventism is that of Ellen White. Her most highly regarded work is found in *The Conflict of the Ages* series, a five-volume narrative commentary on the Bible; and in *Steps to Christ*, a handbook of basic Christian spirituality. The first sentence of the first book in The Conflict series is "God is love." The final sentence of the last book ends with "God is love." Between these two declarations, White works to show love has been the constant, overarching motivation for every act of God. Creation, the call of Abraham, the work of prophets, God's forgiveness of Israel's sins—all were expressions of divine love. Of course. But so were the acts of severity—Noah's flood, the annihilation of the Canaanites, the execution of Uzzah, the Babylonian captivity. White works to persuade us that the sternest of actions attributed to God in the Bible are best explained as divine "tough love."

White begins *Steps to Christ* with a paean to God's love. Spiritual life does not begin with our quest for God or even our hunger for God, but rather with His affectionate regard for us. The first chapter, titled, "God's Love for Man," begins:

"Nature and revelation alike testify of God's love. . . . The sunshine and the rain, that gladden and refresh the earth, the hills and seas and plains, all speak to us of the Creator's love. It is God who supplies the daily needs of all His creatures. . . .

"Yet even amid the suffering that results from sin, God's love is revealed. It is written that God cursed the ground for man's sake (Gen. 3:17). The thorn and the thistle—the difficulties and trials that make his life one of toil and care—were appointed for his good as a part of the training needful in God's plan for his uplifting from the ruin and degradation that sin has wrought. . . .

" 'God is love' is written upon every opening bud, upon every spire of springing grass. The lovely birds making the air vocal with their happy songs, the delicately tinted flowers in their perfection perfuming the air, the lofty trees of the forest with their rich foliage of living green—all testify to the tender, fatherly care of our God and to His desire to make His children happy. . . .

"God has bound our hearts to Him by unnumbered tokens in heaven and in earth. Through the things of nature, and the deepest and tenderest earthly ties that human hearts can know, He has sought to reveal Himself to us. Yet these but imperfectly represent His love" (*Steps to Christ*, pp. 9, 10).

I am citing White in this instance not as a theological authority but as historical evidence. I am not suggesting her words prove God is love. Rather, they are compelling evidence that in Adventist theology, this conviction is foundational.

In recent decades there has been scholarly debate over the precise nature of White's authorship. She made extensive use of copied material and literary assistants. But even if it could be demonstrated that someone other than she was directly responsible for the emphasis on love evident in her most revered works, that would, if anything, strengthen my argument. If we as a community were to assign someone to "write in the prophet's name," we would assign someone whose central conviction was God is love. The statements about God's love in the Ellen White corpus are not mere decoration; they are not epicycles. They are integral to the central themes of the books.

As of 2007, the Seventh-day Adventist creed included 28 doctrinal statements ranging from a declaration that the Bible is the trustworthy revelation of God to a prohibition on smoking. Our church has never formally declared which of our doctrines are most important or most foundational. You could probably find examples of individual Adventists making almost any one of our doctrinal statements central in their thought and practice. Adventists are (to understate it) diverse. But the leading exponents of the major varieties of Adventism would unhesitatingly affirm that the great bedrock truth is God is love. Every other conviction is tested by this conviction.

A distinctive Adventist doctrine is our rejection of the notion of hell as a place of continuous, eternal torment. Adventists adduce a number of Bible passages in support of our belief that hell is an event at the end of time rather than a place of ongoing torment (e.g., Matt. 13:40-42; Rom. 6:23; Rev. 21:5). An increasing number of Protestant biblical scholars publicly teach that the New Testament view of hell is similar to the Adventist doctrine. The Adventist position is certainly strongly supported by the Bible. But, when I trace the history of our rejection of eternal hell, what strikes me is not the force of the specific biblical data but the strength of the intuitive conviction that a God of love could not torture anyone forever. Our quest for biblical evidence against eternal torment was driven by an unshakeable certainty that God is love.

We don't agree on the details of what it means to be loving. We argue about the meaning and appropriateness of "tough love." We discuss the role of community discipline. When does love require the enforcement of ethical and moral boundaries; when does it call for the elimination of social and cultural barriers? We fiercely debate the connection between love and retribution. Does love for the victim require retributive justice or does love for the perpetrator preclude it? But we carry on the debate with the shared assumption that our conclusions must align with our central conviction that God is love.

Adventists usually picture the new earth as being very earthy and real. Instead of clouds and harps, we imagine people talking with God, studying, traveling, building houses, playing with animals. It's not that we really think we know what the new earth will be like, but we are utterly confident God in His love will make our future better than our best imagination. So we playfully imagine, knowing we cannot overstate the richness of God's intentions for our future.

In line with a long Jewish and Christian history, Adventists have given a lot of attention to theodicy—the question of God's justice in the light of human suffering. We vigorously reject one classic resolution of this problem—that God is God and can do whatever He wishes. We insist the final answer to this question cannot turn the assertion that God is love on its head. A key element of the final judgment is a demonstration that these words are true in a way that makes sense to the human mind.

For Adventists the central theme in the human story is God's work to create a community of beings who will love Him and each other. Creation was God's action of "giving birth" as a Parent. All the acts of God, from sending Jesus to save sinners to the decisions of the final judgment, are expressions of love. Even the misery and tragedy of human existence get linked to God's love by interpreting pain and evil as consequences of human abuse of the freedom necessary for genuine love. Eventually, evil and suffering will disappear and God's love will triumph. By means of the judgment process, all humanity will finally be convinced that God could not have done it better. That future is described in the final lines of Ellen White's most famous book:

"And the years of eternity, as they roll, will bring richer and still more glorious revelations of God and of Christ. As knowledge is progressive so will love, reverence, and happiness increase. The more men learn of God, the greater will be their admiration of His character. . . .

"The great controversy is ended. Sin and sinners are no more. The entire universe is clean. One pulse of harmony and gladness beats through the vast creation. From Him who created all, flow life and light and gladness, throughout the realms of illimitable space. From the minutest atom to the greatest world, all things, animate and inanimate, in their unshadowed beauty and perfect joy, declare that God is love" (*The Great Controversy*, p. 678).

This is the first Adventist conviction.

Apophaticism

*"For my thoughts are not your thoughts, neither are your ways my ways,"
declares the Lord. "As the heavens are higher than the earth, so are my
ways higher than your ways and my thoughts than your thoughts"
(Isa. 55:8, 9, NIV).*

Theologians in the Eastern Orthodox tradition have developed an approach to theology called apophaticism. Apophaticism is the conviction that humans cannot really make any meaningful affirmation about God because of the limitations of human language and understanding. For example, if I say God is love, that would be a false statement because my understanding of love is so meager and defective that my words distort more than they inform.* Apophaticism expresses the truth that human language is inadequate to voice the full truth about God.

However, in our primary source for religious knowledge, the Bible, the prophets, and the writers are very bold in their use of human language. They acknowledge that God is beyond human speech and understanding, but still insist we can make meaningful statements about God. They even put human words in God's mouth. "But now, this is what the Lord says—he who created you, O Jacob, he who formed you, O Israel: 'Fear not, for I have redeemed you; I have summoned you by name; you are mine'" (Isa. 43:1, NIV).

Perhaps the most dramatic use of human language to describe God is found in Exodus 34:6, 7: "The Lord passed in front of Moses proclaiming, 'The Lord, the Lord, the compassionate and gracious God, slow to anger, abounding in love and faithfulness, maintaining love to thousands, and forgiving wickedness, rebellion and sin. Yet he does not leave the guilty unpunished; he punishes the children and their children for the sin of the fathers to the third and fourth generation'" (NIV).

This passage highlights the power of language and its limits. Here Moses quotes God as if He was using human words. God claims to have attributes we humans can understand—compassion and patience, etc. God is also pictured as sending punishment onto successive generations. Elsewhere in Scripture, this concept of God is specifically corrected

(Eze. 18). Scholars offer various interpretations of these words about the punishment of the sins of the fathers. The language is problematic. But just because language (and cultural conditioning) creates difficulties, we cannot ignore the power of language to connect people with the realities of God.

One of the principle ways in which the Bible attempts to communicate what God is like is through metaphor. "God is like . . ." And the most powerful metaphor is anthropomorphism; that is, using human categories to describe God. God is father, mother, shepherd, lover. He has eyes, hands, and a voice. He raises His strong arm in our defense. He repents (or relents), and feels the emotions of love, jealousy, hope.

The use of these human traits to help us understand God is more art than science, but who would argue that science does a better job in interpersonal communication than art? And the point of the Bible is personal communication.

If God is the Creator, then we can expect that creation will point back to its Maker. If, as the Bible clearly teaches, humanity is God's magnum opus, then we would expect human experience, in a special way, to point toward God. The Bible acknowledges that creation and human nature have been deranged by sin. We do not see a one-to-one correspondence between the natural world and what is true in the supernatural reality of God. But while the correspondence is not precise, it is real. We can know something of God by extrapolating from earthly realities.

From our capacities to reason, create, make music, love, paint, construct, design, emote, judge, evaluate, etc., we confidently infer something of what God is like. When the Bible writers use human language to talk about God, we confidently assume that there is some correspondence between the human words and the divine realities being described. Of course, the human words do not precisely and comprehensively state the divine reality, but it is not necessary for us to be able to speak exhaustively and absolutely about God in order to speak meaningfully and truthfully about Him.

Apophaticism is a valuable reminder of the limitations of humanity. It stands as a proper rebuke of our natural arrogance when we are propounding our particular understanding of what God is like. But if it assumes too large a role in our theology, it will interfere with our proper obedience to the command of Jesus, "Go and teach all nations" and will diminish our confidence in the testimony of John, "Everyone who loves is born of God and knows God" (1 John 4:7, NKJV).

We are called to communicate to the world the message of God's passionate love. To do that, we have to join the Bible writers in using human language and the metaphors of human relationships in speaking of God. Let's be as unabashed as the Bible and pray that we are half as effective.

---

* See Jaroslav Pelikan, *The Christian Tradition: A History of the Development of Doctrine, Volume 2: The Spirit of Eastern Christendom (600-1700).*

Father God

But when you pray, do not use vain repetitions like the heathen, who think that they will be heard because of their many words. Do not pray like them because your Father knows what you need before you ask Him. So pray like this: "Our Father who is in heaven" (Matt. 6:7-9).

Sally stopped me as I walked up East 87th Street toward my office at Church of the Advent Hope. We visited a few minutes. Then, almost visibly gathering her courage, she said, "Could I make a request? Could you quit using the word 'father' in your sermons? Every time you say that word I don't hear another thing you say for the next five minutes, sometimes 10. Father is a curse word to me."

Sally went on to sketch a heartbreaking story of abuse. Church had not been part of her life until recently. Now she was seeking God and hoping that church might help her in that quest. But there was nothing in the word "father" that attracted her to God. So, when I as a preacher talked about God as "Father" in an effort to paint a picture of a reliable provider, a strong defender, a ready source of mercy and compassion, it took awhile for her to compose herself enough to listen to me again. As a pastor, I have heard too many stories of failed fathers. Bill's dad was unfaithful to his wife and utterly unavailable to his children. John's father was given to capricious, terrifying violence. Martha's father used ridicule and scorn. The stories that trouble me most are about clergy fathers.

Brianna is the daughter of a nationally-known evangelist. Others have told me in glowing terms of his positive impact on their lives. But with Brianna he was alternately hostile and remote. In her 20s, she was struggling to find wholeness and hope beyond the misshapen image of God bequeathed to her from Daddy.

Then there was Susy. Her father was a well-known and beloved Adventist theologian. I've heard his former students speak glowingly of the warmth and verisimilitude of his lectures about Jesus. He touched thousands of lives with hope and conviction. But his boomer daughter still struggles with an ineradicable sense of unworthiness. She was never, never, ever good enough to please her father. If he had been a scoundrel, perhaps she could have learned to do without his smile, but he was a godly man, highly respected in the church. For Susy, his disapproval became the face of God. God is the unpleasable father. Father is a very heavy word.

But Jesus said, "When you pray, say, "'Our Father. . . .'"

One way to deal with the fact of paternal failure is to dismiss fathers as unnecessary for our theology. We can construct theology by using gender-neutral terms: "Our Parent in heaven . . ." Or we can attempt to be more sophisticated and dismiss parental images of God altogether as crude gropings after a spiritual reality that is best understood without resorting to primitive anthropomorphism. "O Great One. . . ." "Eternal Spirit. . . ."

But I don't think either of these approaches would prove beneficial. The stories of failed fathers that I hear are always associated with psychosocial and spiritual damage to the children. And a deep, ineradicable hunger. Dad's face becomes the face of God, the face of the universe. If I know myself to be loved by Dad, the universe is a friendly place. God is a gracious deity. However, if I could never please Dad, I will find it very difficult to believe that God smiles when He looks in my direction. And we can't simply learn to do without Dad's smile. We are driven to find an adequate replacement.

Often these "replacement fathers" take us deeper into dysfunction. Pathological sexual relationships, chemical addictions, and workaholism often are fueled by our desperate hunger for something to take the place of what we should have received from Dad. Even religion can deepen and intensify our dysfunction. The natural tendency is to project onto God the brokenness of our fathers. So God becomes unpleasable, aloof, severe, arbitrary and authoritarian, capricious, careless, faithless. Men copy the brokenness of their fathers and think they are acting like God.

But God has something better in mind. We are invited to look beyond the distortions of God that come to us from our families of origin. God wants us to see the real character of God as described in the teachings of Jesus in the sixth chapter of Matthew: "Your Father, who sees what you do in private, will reward you. . . . Your Father already knows what you need before you ask him. Look at the birds . . . your Father takes care of them! Aren't you worth much more than birds? . . . It is God who clothes the wild grass. . . . Won't He be all the more sure to clothe you? Do not worry, saying, 'What will I eat?' or 'What will I wear?' Your Father in heaven knows that you need all these things . . . and He will provide you with them" (vs. 6-33).

Jesus portrays God as an idealized human father. He is responsive and affirming, aware, not aloof or absent. He actively provides for us. He takes note of our noble deeds and rewards them. He delights in doing us good.

"Fear not, little flock. It is your Father's good pleasure to give you the kingdom" (Luke 12:32).

Full maturity comes to us as we move from relying for our identity on the imperfect reflection of God exhibited by our earthly fathers to reliance on God as He really is. For many people this kind of maturity does not come easily (to understate it wildly). So God has called the church to help people grow into this kind of maturity. Through the church God intends to offer human models to help us imagine divine realities. In the church we are to know ourselves as loved, supported, exhorted, taught, disciplined, treasured. When the church approaches this ideal, it becomes a healing community. It gives meaning to the biblical phrase, "the household of God."

Like a Mother

*O Jerusalem, Jerusalem. You kill the prophets and stone the messengers
I send to you. How often I have longed to embrace you and gather you to
myself as a mother hen gathers her chicks under her wings. But you would
not let me! (see Matt. 23:37).*

*Can a nursing mother forget her baby and fail to care for her newborn?
In truth, she will forget before I forget you (see Isa. 49:15).*

In the late 1990s in Oxnard, California, a 50-year-old man was tried and
convicted for the shooting death of a police officer. The accused was a
drifter, always in and out of trouble. He was broken, mentally ill, deranged
from years of drinking and drugs. There was no question about who did
it. There was some question about why. But in the end there was no
answer to that question. There was not even a whiff of improper police
conduct. It appeared to be an utterly senseless killing. A heartbreaking case
of a policeman showing up in the wrong place at the wrong time, and a
deranged man who decided to shoot him.

The police officer's family was wrenched beyond words. The officer
was in his 30s, with a young wife and children. Their trauma was appropriately highlighted in news about the shooting and in the lead-up to the
trial.

Wilma Johnson sat silently in the courtroom through every day of the
trial. She listened to the prosecutor describe the crime. She heard the victim's family describe the raw pain that hounded their lives. She sensed the
community outrage.

A reporter talked to Mrs. Johnson after the trial. She said she understood the anger of the family and the outrage of the community. She, too,
was appalled by the crime, by the loss. The killer deserved to pay for his
crime, she said. What he did was monstrously evil. She did not, for even
a second, excuse what he had done. She ached for the grieving family.

But there was one other fact that she wanted the world to know. This
broken, deranged murderer was also her son. He might be a son that only
a mother could love, but she was a mother and he was her son. She wanted
the world to know that, too.

God loves His children like that—the good ones and the bad ones, the stars and the ne'er-do-wells. He does not excuse evil. He's not soft on sin. But nothing can ever change the fact that He claims you as His own. No matter whom you've hurt, no matter what you've done, He loves you. He always will.

God is a realist. He stares unblinkingly at the reality of evil. There are people who, knowing good and evil, choose evil. There are people who make bad choices, not because they are confused or misled, but because they cultivate an active preference for something evil. These people will not enjoy eternity with God. But even though their exclusion from eternity is right, and even in their best interest, God's heart will ache for them.

The more intimately acquainted we become with the tenacity of God's affection, the softer our own hearts will become toward the broken and perverse, and the more stubborn we will be in hoping for and praying for those who appear to be citizens of hell.

God's Dogs

*"But God has now brought you to life with Christ. God forgave us all our
sins; he canceled the unfavorable record of our debts with its binding
rules and did away with it completely by nailing it to the cross"
(Col. 2:13, 14, TEV).*

A parks department official knocked at our front door. Did we have a
brown dog? Yes. Well, all the garbage cans in the park had been tipped
over and garbage had been strewn around. Witnesses said the culprit was
our brown dog. And, the parks official continued, this was not the first
time. If we did not keep our dog in we would face a hefty fine and the
dog would be confiscated.

I apologized profusely and promised to do two things: to try harder to
keep the dog in and to clean the park, whether Toby or another animal
trashed it. Turns out it was much easier to keep the second promise.

Toby was an escape artist. He would dig under the fence on the park
side of my lawn in spite of my efforts with rocks, logs, and fill dirt to make
digging out impossible. (We shared about 500 feet of fence with the park.)
He would climb over the fence on the opposite side of the yard and circle
the block to the park. For several months, he pushed his way through a
gate whose fastening had a slight give in it. After the kids discovered his
trick, I strengthened the gate. Sometimes, for a while after one of my fixes,
Toby would be confined. A month or two would pass, then I would again
be summoned by scratching at the front door. And there he would be
standing, grinning and happy about his feast in the park, ready to be welcomed home.

I would take him through the house to the backyard, put him in his
kennel, and head to the park to pick up trash. What a mess! Dirty diapers.
McDonald's bags with ketchup and food smeared on the outside. Cigarette
butts. Paper plates coated with food on both sides. Napkins. Soda bottles
and cans. Wrappers. Watermelon rinds.

Even at home Toby was no angel. For a year after we first brought him
home from the pound, he terrorized our cats. He ate the neighbor's chinchilla. We faced several options. We could disown him or have him put

down. Or we could claim him, discipline him over and over until he left the cats alone, apologize to the neighbors about the chinchilla and clean up the park. You already know what I did. Toby was my dog. His problems were mine.

We are God's dogs. We have made huge, horrid messes, and they cannot be tolerated. God could disown us. He could put us down. Instead, He claims our messes as His own. Even when others cannot handle our behavior, He still claims us as His own. Even when we have created a moral indebtedness that we can never repay—and maybe to which we are utterly oblivious—God still pays.

Theologians have long wrestled with how to make logical sense of Bible statements that the crucifixion of Christ ransomed sinners or paid their debt. Scholarly inquiry is useful, but it might help us make intuitive sense of this language if we thought of ourselves as God's dogs. And if you're offended by the comparison, you haven't paid enough attention to what humans are up to lately.

Divine Grief

"Can a woman forget the baby at her breast and have no compassion on the child she has borne? Though she may forget,I will not forget you!" (Isa. 49:15, NIV).

I had been in my new church just a few weeks and was making my rounds, getting acquainted with my church members. It was not very many minutes into my visit with Lois when she began telling me about the great hole in her life left by the death of her daughter, Angela. Her grief was sharp and fresh, as though Angela had died just the day before.

I listened closely as details spilled out. Angela had drowned. She had been a beautiful girl—sweet, thoughtful. It was a hot summer day. She and some friends had gone to the lake.

It did not quite make sense to me. The way Lois talked, I was sure the accident had occurred only a short time ago. But Angela sounded like a teenager. And Lois was 80 years old. Finally, Lois mentioned the detail I had been listening for. Angela had died on her sixteenth birthday, 40 years before.

A mother's heart does not forget. Her grief does not go away.

According to popular Christian teaching, when someone dies he or she goes immediately into the presence of God or enters the torments of hell. According to this view, before our death God is limited in His interaction with us by the illusions and frailty of our bodily existence. However, when a believer dies, death heals this separation and leads immediately to the joy of unhindered spiritual fellowship between God and His child. So for God, death is a great boon. It is the door to heaven. We who are left on earth may be wracked by grief but God's heart is gladdened by the homeward flight of His child.

The Adventist understanding of what happens when people die paints an entirely different picture of God. When someone dies, the person stops interacting with God through prayer, worship, and obedience. Certainly the person is not lost to the heart or memory of God. But as an active, thinking, loving, talking human being, the person no longer exists. In the language of the Bible, the person sleeps (John 11:11-14). A dead person has no awareness of time or waiting. The person remains unconscious until the resurrection. At the Second Coming all of God's people are united and taken en masse into the presence of God. They all arrive at the heavenly party together (Heb. 11:39, 40).

In this view, God Himself is deprived of the living companionship of a person who dies—just as are the grieving family and friends. Instead of death being a boon to God, death robs God of the worship of His people (Ps. 115:17). When people die, the heavenly Father no longer hears the voices of His children in praise and prayer. He has memories to cherish and a future to anticipate, but He is not in fellowship with their vital, interactive "souls."

In the story of Lazarus, who was a close personal friend of Jesus, we read that moments before He raised Lazarus from the dead, Jesus wept. Given Jesus' divinity, this incident portrays God's identification with human pain. Jesus knew that Lazarus was not going to remain dead. Still, the heartbreak of His friends brought Jesus Himself to tears. It is a truism that when children hurt, their moms and dads hurt as much as or more than the young one. And God, our heavenly Parent, hurts for His children. When grief batters our hearts and wets our eyes, God hurts because we hurt. But there is more to God's grief than that.

God's grief is not only the response of His heart to the arrows of pain that wound us. God Himself is wounded by the separation caused by death. Death interrupts God's own conversation with His child. God bears the emotional cost of the system He has designed. When it comes to enduring pain, God asks nothing of us that He does not require of Himself.

This perspective of God as a grieving parent has large implications for how we view the delay of the Advent. Why hasn't Jesus returned as He promised? What's taking so long? Explanations include: God is waiting because He wants to save more people. He is waiting for some predetermined time. He's waiting for evil to reach its full flower or for the gospel to be preached in all the world or for the character of Christ to be perfectly reproduced in His people.

Each of these theories has something to recommend it, and each has problems. The Adventist understanding of the nature of death does not answer the question, Why does God wait? It does, however, change the emotional content of the question. In addition to asking why God doesn't hurry up and rescue us from our trouble (a very good and proper question), this picture of God's grief prompts us to ask, Why doesn't God spare Himself? If the redeemed are sleeping, awaiting the great resurrection morning described so vividly in the New Testament, then every day God delays the Second Coming is another day He carries the wounds of a bereaved parent. Since God loves every human more intensely than a mother loves her only child, the Adventist understanding of death is a picture of a brokenhearted God.

In the traditional view of death, there is little motivation for God to bring human history to an end. Every day God is welcoming children home. But in the Adventist view, every day that passes adds to the grief that weighs on God's heart. God does not ask us to bear burdens He Himself does not carry. He does not encourage us to be brave in the face of pain that He Himself does not feel.

I remember listening to a sermon at a funeral in Akron, Ohio. On the front row were four or five kids, siblings of an 8-year-old boy who had been killed when the front wheel of his bicycle hit a rock and he was thrown in front of a passing car.

The preacher spoke directly to the young people on the front row. "Try not to take your brother's death too hard. I know you miss him, but God needed him up in heaven and that's why He took him. God must have some very important job in mind for your brother up there. Stay close to Jesus and some day you'll join your brother in heaven, and he'll show you around the New Jerusalem and tell you all about what he's been doing while you were down here working for Jesus."

The pastor was doing what a pastor is supposed to do—mining the spiritual and theological resources of his community for all the comfort and solace he could find. But I was appalled at the implications of his words.

So are you telling me, I imagined shouting, that every time God runs low on kitchen help in the heavenly cafeteria He throws rocks in front of little kids' bike tires? Is God really that hard up for help in heaven? What kind of God is that?

This view, if true, would mean our deepest wounds bring great joy to God. People who are the most lovable and leave the greatest emptiness here on earth when they die bring instant joy in the courts of heaven. We on earth bear all the cost of improving heaven's work force.

The popular view of death does offer some comfort. It places those who have died in a good place far from all pain (though logically, the joy of heaven would be tainted by the awareness that back on earth there are loved ones still exposed to evil and suffering).

In truth, when the believer dies, the very next moment in their experience will be the resurrection and the presence of God. The time in the grave that is felt all too keenly by grieving survivors does not exist in the experience of the one who has died.

The Adventist understanding of death addresses the reality of pain confronted by those who are still alive. For those who survive the death of a loved one, the immediate reality is grief and hurt. And in every death, one of the survivors, one of the mourners, is God Himself. There is no benefit for God in the death of His children. He is not knocking off children to fill the heavenly kitchens or choirs. He does not forget our grief in the great joy of His communion with His children who have escaped from their earthly prisons into His presence. Instead, God enters the very depths of our grief. In fact, our purest, deepest grief is but a faint reflection of God's grief. If we are able to receive it, the pain of our grief is a stern education about the depth and intensity of God's love.

The Holy Family

So you are no longer foreigners and aliens but fellow citizens with God's people and members of God's household (see Eph. 2:19).

I was 22 years old, headed from Memphis to Pacific Union College as a transfer student for my senior year. I had never been to the school and didn't know a soul there. I got off the plane in Oakland and waded into the sea of unknown faces in the terminal, looking for Uncle Ellsworth. I had met him only once before, when I was 6 years old, so I didn't have the slightest idea what he looked like. But a tall man with a mane of white hair and a kindly face approached and greeted me tentatively. "John?"

Within seconds, I went from being a stranger lost in a crowded airport to a long-lost son coming home. Uncle Ellsworth and Aunt Bernice embraced me with warm affection. My cousin Jeanine proved to be a wonderful friend, offering sage "sisterly advice" regarding girls and dating. Aunt Bernice's spaghetti on Friday night was the highlight of each week. Here in this new place among new people, I found myself at home because I was family.

Americans celebrate the individual. Our national stories honor individuals who have risen above their family origins and through hard work and initiative have achieved individual greatness. Most of us know nothing of Ben Franklin's family, or George Washington's, for that matter. We are suspicious of political dynasties such as the Kennedys or Bushes. We wonder if the younger members of the families have attained office because of family connections. And there is no compliment intended in the question. Some protest affirmative action as a political agenda because they believe it devalues individual achievement.

But in reality, personal identity is not created ex nihilo by individuals. It is given by family, either literal or figurative. Individuals make real choices and shape themselves through choices that become habits and character. But all of this activity of the will is at most a mere remod-

29

eling of identities given us by our families. Identity is a gift more than an achievement. This perspective is pervasive throughout the Bible.

In the beginning, humanity's identity was the gift of creation—we were created in the image of God. The story of the Jews celebrates the status they enjoyed as descendants of Abraham. The Bible highlights privileges that were theirs as members of the nation that God had chosen quite apart from the character or characteristics of the individual (or even of the community at any one point in time [see Deut. 7:7]). In the New Testament, believers are not pictured as saved individuals but as beloved members of the holy family, the household of God.

When the Old Testament affirms God's regard for non-Jewish people, it does so by picturing them as honorary members of the Jewish community. Consider the stories of Rahab, Ruth, and Naaman (Matt. 1; Josh. 2; Ruth 1-4; 2 Kings 5) and the inclusive language of Psalm 87 (NEB): "The Lord loves the gates of Zion . . . and he has made her his home. He says, 'I will make her my home. I will count Egypt and Babylon among my friends; Philistine, Tyrian, and Nubian will be there; and Zion shall be called a mother in whom men of every race are born.' The Lord will write against each in the roll of the nations: 'This one was born in her.'"

Notice that Babylonians and Philistines, traditional enemies of the Jews, who receive the favor of the Lord are not honored as the noblest citizens of their respective lands. Instead they are received as honorary citizens of Jerusalem. They are reckoned as members of the earthly community that receives God's favor.

This theme echoes throughout the New Testament as well. The story is told of an encounter between Jesus and Zacchaeus, a tax collector in the city of Jericho. In that society, tax collectors had the social standing of drug dealers in our society—envied for their wealth, despised for their wickedness. Because they worked with the Roman occupation forces, they were seen as traitorous collaborators and regarded as hopelessly corrupt.

Jesus invited Himself to Zacchaeus' house for dinner. At the table, Zacchaeus announces he is giving away half his money to the poor and that he will repay anyone he has cheated four times what he stole. Jesus responds to this evidence of transformation by announcing, "Today salvation has come to this house, because this man, too, is a son of Abraham. For the Son of Man came to seek and to save the lost" (Luke 19:9, 10).

Notice, Jesus describes Zacchaeus' new status not in terms of his individual, personal connection with God, but in terms of his restoration to citizenship in the community of Abraham (a figure of speech for the people of God).

The Bible says very little about "God and me." Its emphasis is "God and we." Salvation is not something that I achieve through the pursuit of personal holiness; it is the gift of inclusion in the holy community. The blessings enjoyed by a follower of Jesus are gifts to the chosen people, the holy nation—that is, the church. They are not given to holy individuals—except as those individuals are incorporated into the people of God.

The book of Revelation brings this emphasis on community to a climax. In chapter 3 Jesus is pictured as knocking at the door, seeking to enjoy dinner with individuals ("I will go in and eat with him and he with Me"). But more frequently in Revelation, the focus is on the people of God, gathered from "every tribe, nation, kindred people," whom Jesus has anointed as priests (Revelation 1). They form a heavenly chorus and "follow the Lamb wherever He goes." They sit on thrones with their compatriots, judging and reigning forever (Rev. 5, 7, 20, 22). Salvation is enjoyed by the host of God's people in corporate worship and reigning with God, not by individuals in private, one-on-one interaction with Him.

The theme song of heaven is not "I Come to the Garden Alone" but "Shall We Gather at the River?"

This communal source of identity is celebrated in the central practices of the Christian church—baptism, communion, Sabbathkeeping. It is associated with most of the classic explications of the crucifixion of Jesus. It has profound implications for our understanding of the church and is inseparable from our doctrine of God.

Historically, we Adventists have seen ourselves as uniquely called to serve as God's church at the end of time. This belief can be distorted into spiritual arrogance, but properly understood it highlights the essential role of community in the work of God. God is not looking for spiritual Lone Rangers to show up here and there and perform heroic deeds for the kingdom of heaven. Rather, God is looking for people who are willing to participate in building a holy community, a society known for its faith, hope, and love. Spiritual life is something we build together. It is not something we achieve alone.

To those who are vividly aware of their inadequacies or failings, God offers the gift of membership in His household. You do not have to earn your place or prove your merit or fight your way in. You merely say yes to the invitation. To people who see themselves as foreigners and strangers, God gives the assurance that He has set a place for them at the family table.

To those who hesitate to associate with the riffraff whom Jesus sometimes attracts, the reality of church offers a strong check on pride.

We readily recognize certain kinds of human ability as gifts—things such as musical ability or high IQ. We have a harder time recognizing personal drive, motivation, and moral and spiritual sensitivity as gifts. But

God, in calling us to His table, reminds us that none of us arrive there by spontaneous generation. We were birthed and re-birthed. (And no one births himself.) All of our abilities were gifts before they became achievements. And all of our failings were first weaknesses and wounds that came to us apart from our will.

One of the crucial functions of the church is to actively welcome others into full participation in the life of the holy family. As the family of Jesus, the church is obliged to seek and save the lost. These lost ones may be crushed with feelings of inadequacy or swollen with self-confidence, but they equally need the accountability and affirmation that comes from participation in the earthly family of God.

Our most precious identity is the one that is given to us irrespective of our accomplishment or demerit. The greatest benefits we receive come because of the resources of the family, not because of our own personal achievements. When we step off the plane, we are greeted by Uncle Ellsworth and taken home because we are family. And we will be welcomed into heaven at last, not because we have mastered faith or spiritual habits or conquered our addictions and dysfunction, but because we are members of the household of God.

Every family has traditions, specific habits and practices that develop over time as they live together. Some are mere preferences. Others are utterly essential for family well-being. In the church we also have traditions. Some are mere preferences—such as times and styles of music for worship services. Others are utterly crucial—such as reverence for the Bible and obedience to Jesus.

The next four chapters describe spiritual traditions that are important to Adventists. They are not unique to our church, but they have a prominent place in our life together. We don't pretend our way of life is the only way to be authentically Christian. But we unabashedly claim this way of life as a treasured heritage and an authentic form of Christian practice. These practices are useful to us as we seek to cultivate a vital connection with God and to serve our neighbors. They help us to be more effective in carrying forward the ministry Jesus has assigned us. We find this way of life precious and welcome others to experience it with us.

Memory Verses and Daily Worship

"Thy word is a lamp unto my feet, and a light unto my path"
(Ps.119:105, KJV).

My congregation recently launched a new worship service targeting families with elementary school-age children. As we talked together about what elements to include in the service, one of the first to be included was a weekly memory verse. At each service we would recite together a verse that had been assigned for memory work the previous week.

This carries forward one of the most central of Christian convictions: God has spoken in the Bible and one of the primary ways to cultivate spiritual life is to cultivate deep acquaintance with the Bible.

For as far back as I can remember, memorization of passages in the Bible has been an essential element of children's programs. By the time I entered high school I had been coached in memorizing hundreds of Bible verses.

During my freshman year of college, a preacher came for a week of sermons. Morris Venden talked slowly. He made it sound so easy to enjoy God's favor and experience salvation that I was sure he was a heretic. (I had grown up believing it nearly impossible to gain God's favor.) I continued to listen, and as I did I found him persuasive. But as significant as the theological content of his preaching was, Venden's greatest impact on my life and on the lives of thousands of others was his emphasis on a particular habit, a spiritual practice.

He described his own tormented quest for a vital connection with God. When he was a young preacher, someone had called him for help. This person wanted to know one thing—Did he know God? Could he help her get to know God? Of course, as a seminary-educated preacher, Venden had a lot of information about God—he could explain theology. But he wasn't sure he knew God personally. He launched a desperate search. Eventually he concluded that spiritual life boiled down to three things: Read your Bible every day, pray, and tell others what you discover in the first two activities. Venden wanted us to spend an hour a day reading and meditating on the Bible.

Of course, an hour a day was impossible for me as a college student, but then I met other students who mentioned that they were trying it. They reported that it made a difference in their lives. I figured that if they could do it, so could I. And I did. Over the decades, spending time most mornings reading and meditating on the Bible has profoundly shaped my spiritual life. When I talk with other people in my demographic—people who were young adults in the 70s and were influenced by the preaching of Morris Venden, I have heard repeated affirmations of the power of this advice. Spending time daily in interacting with the words of the Bible is a powerful aid in the cultivation of a rich spiritual life.

Which translation is the best? Occasionally I meet people who argue that one particular translation is the best. But the church has long taught a simple answer to this question: The best translation is the one you read and understand. God's presence in the words of Scripture is so real, so radiant, it will shine through any translation you invest time in with a desire to meet God.

How can you be sure you are getting the "real truth" inasmuch as there are so many translations? Two points: 1. The important stuff is affirmed in multiple passages throughout the Bible. So you don't ever have to depend exclusively on the precise words of any one particular verse. You find the "real truth" by reading the Bible as a whole, not by collecting obscure, complicated passages. 2. When you look at the translations as a whole there is actually very little difference between them. Not only does God's presence shine through all the translations, so does God's truth.

No translation is absolutely perfect, since they have all passed through the minds of flawed human beings. Adventists make no claim that even the original Hebrew, Aramaic, and Greek words were inerrant in the usual American Protestant sense. But that poses no problem because the purpose of the Bible is not to give us flawless information but to bring us into a vital connection with God. One of my friends, Ernie Ford, likes to say, "The Bible is not a book; it is a place." As we read, we are entering the presence of God. We are in a good place to hear His voice. The ultimate purpose of reading, memorizing, and meditating on the Bible is not mastery of its words and ideas but engagement with God and service to people.

So we continue to assign memory verses in our Sabbath morning Bible classes for all ages. And we continue to exhort one another to give daily attention to the words of the Bible.

Sabbath in Zion

Then they came to Capernaum and on the Sabbath they entered the synagogue where he taught. . . . After they left the synagogue, they went to the home of Simon and Andrew (see Mark 1:21, 29).

We were supposed to leave Los Angeles on Thursday morning for a long weekend in Zion National Park. But when I called Pep Boys late Wednesday afternoon, the mechanic reported that our van was still co-matose. Thursday afternoon brought no improvement. Friday at about noon, my wife and I crammed kids and camping gear into our Subaru and 11 hours later, after stops for restrooms, gas, food, and restrooms again, we arrived at the park. The campground was silent and dark. Scouting the message board I found the promised note: "Griswolds are in campsite 34; we've registered you in site 35." I turned off my headlights and with the amber glow of the parking lights we found our site, pitched our tent, and slept.

Sabbath morning at breakfast we met the others—the Bryants and their college-age kids, the Griswolds and their youngsters, and Bill Jackson and his two boys. Strangers meeting in Zion. After breakfast we loaded into cars and headed down to the Virgin River where we found a spot for church. We sang and talked about the Creator and Redeemer while watching the sun play on the massive formations around us. After a vegetarian lunch we climbed Angel's Landing, a breathtaking pinnacle. At the top we met a group of college kids, one of whom was a drama student. There against the backdrop of stone and immense blue space he recited a poem for us with astonishing pathos and eloquence.

Late that afternoon the group scattered across a landscape of cross-bedded sandstone, the younger kids scampering here and there like squirrels, older kids, women, and men drifting into little groups here and there for conversation. The men chewed on questions that arise at the intersection of geology and theology. We talked the afternoon away, luxuriating in the social and spiritual space created by our Sabbath habits.

It was not a gathering of like minds in the sense of sharing common educations—our group included a geologist, an engineer, an entomologist, a theologian—and not in the sense of shared opinions about how and when Creation happened. But we did share a haunting sense of the paucity of our knowledge and a deep appreciation for the complexity and beauty of nature.

Sabbath was the wordless sacrament that created common ground for us, not by dictating our paleontological opinions, but by offering an opportunity to cultivate wonder, awe, humility, and quietness. Sabbath linked us men to one another and to the community of women and college kids and youngsters.

For people whose theology is characterized more by questions than by confidence, Sabbath provides a way to participate deeply in the community of faith. Through walks in the park, shared meals with fellow believers, and community worship, Sabbath provides a concrete way for intellectuals to practice believing. Sabbath practices—Friday night meal rituals, attendance at church, walks in the park, campouts filled with an awareness of God's presence and favor—provide a "bodily" way for us to honor God and confess our own incompleteness, frailty, and evil. By keeping Sabbath we worship.

Sabbath is the most visible of a collection of distinctly Adventist habits—eating vegetarian, abstaining from alcohol, making prudish choices regarding videos and movies, counting 10 percent of our income as God's. In these and other traditions, we find a pattern for living as believers in spite of our doubts. It offers a wholesome form of religious life that we can teach our children without having to answer all their questions about the formal beliefs and institutions of Adventism or Christianity.

We don't claim everything we do is unambiguously commanded by Scripture or that our beliefs and norms are flawlessly consistent. Rather, we claim that our community has grown in the soil of Scripture. We honor the work God has done in the larger communities of Christianity and Judaism as members of those communities that have studied the Bible through the centuries. They have been our mentors as we have developed our own distinctive norms through 150-plus years of reading the Bible and seeking God—together.

Healthful Living

Then the Lord God said, "I give you every seed-bearing plant on the face of the whole earth and every tree that has fruit with seed in it. They will be yours for food" (see Gen. 1:29).

Many Adventists in North America are vegetarians. Not that the majority of Adventists strictly avoid meat, but vegetarianism is our ideal, and we honor that ideal by not serving meat in our community meals. Vegetarianism as a specific practice is linked with several ideals. First, it is rooted in a vision of peace and harmony that is God's plan for our future. As the prophet Isaiah described it, " 'The wolf and the lamb shall feed together. The lion shall eat straw like the ox, and dust shall be the serpent's food. They shall not hurt nor destroy in all My holy mountain,' says the Lord" (Isa. 65:25, NKJV).

If this is our destiny, it makes sense to begin now to practice peaceful living. Vegetarianism is a way of walking lightly in the world. It is a social application of the wilderness ethos of minimal impact on the environment. Calories from commercial meat production appear to carry a much higher environmental cost than an equal amount of food from vegetarian sources.

Vegetarianism also grows out of our conviction that body care is a moral issue. We view our bodies as masterpieces of divine art and temples for the activity of the Holy Spirit, therefore we have a moral obligation to safeguard our health. Eating nutritious food, exercising, getting adequate sleep, and other health practices are seen as essential elements of the normal Christian life. And public instruction regarding healthful practices is a normal part of our church life. The result of this emphasis on healthful living is increased longevity and decreased incidence of disease among Adventists who follow healthy practices.

Our advocacy of wholesome food goes beyond a concern for biological health. There is a substrata of inchoate conviction that abstinence from Twinkies and McDonald's is somehow more congruent with radical moral and ethical purity. Smoking is not just unhealthy; it is "unclean."

We are teetotallers. This is not altogether driven by any particular biblical statement about the evils of alcohol, but by the principle of love for our neighbor. Our church family includes many from ethnic groups that have been devastated by rampant alcoholism. Given the horrific personal, domestic, and social costs of alcoholism, almost anything we can do to help people with a genetic or social propensity toward excessive drinking is worth doing. Our obligation to our friends far outweighs the putative cardiac benefits of moderate wine consumption. Saving marriages and jobs is worth the cost of foregoing the pleasures of social drinking and the cultural pretensions of the wine world.

This carefulness, this abstemiousness, is carried over into our consumption of entertainment. Just as we are careful about what we eat, so we are careful about what we watch and read and play. We teach people that they are responsible for input into their spiritual systems. We encourage members to actively seek esthetic, intellectual, and recreational input that will foster spiritual sensitivity and faithfulness.

We know our eternal destiny is not determined by attention to food, holy days, and environmental stewardship, or by abstinence from tobacco and other drugs. But as parents and friends, spouses and neighbors, we are committed to building a community that promotes personal and social well-being here and now as well as preparing people for the hereafter. As disciples of Jesus, we aim to help each other and the larger world cultivate health in every area of life—physical, social, spiritual. As we practice healthy ways of living we become more available for down-to-earth service in Jesus' name.

Jesus said that He came so that people could experience life and experience it more abundantly (John 10:10). He came to set people free and to offer healing (Luke 4:18). In our attention to health and social issues, we are simply following the example and teachings of Jesus.

Saying Grace

"The eyes of all are lifted to thee in hope. Thou givest them their food when it is due. With open and bountiful hand Thou satisfieth the desire of every living creature." (Ps. 145:15, 16, NEB).

Bill and I pushed our way into a crowded eatery in West Yellowstone on the last day of a geology field trip. We ordered our sandwiches—he, a hamburger with the works; and I, avocado, cucumber, and sprouts on nine-grain bread. Our food was delivered. Bill picked up his hamburger and began devouring it. I paused for a second to say grace and then began inhaling my sandwich. After we had taken the edge off our hunger, I eyed the professor, then laughingly accused him. "Bill, you left out the human part of eating that hamburger."

Bill didn't get it at first. He thought I was teasing him for his carnivorous lunch, but that wasn't it. "You ate that sandwich the way my dog would have. You forgot to say thanks." Bill grudgingly acknowledged the rebuke.

Saying grace (or thanks or the blessing) at meals is a way to turn eating into a spiritual exercise. In this pause for prayer we bring some of the holiness of the Lord's Supper into our ordinary experience. Ellen White wrote, "To the death of Christ we owe even this earthly life. The bread we eat is the purchase of His broken body. The water we drink is bought by His spilled blood. Never one, saint or sinner, eats his daily food, but he is nourished by the body and the blood of Christ. The cross of Calvary is stamped on every loaf" (*The Desire of Ages*, p. 660).

This is perhaps the most widespread of all spiritual practices. Nearly every spiritual tradition teaches people to regard food as a gift and to cultivate that awareness by offering a prayer before eating. In our contemporary world of fast food it is easy to lose this reverence for food. We get our food from the take-out window while we are talking on our cell phones. We eat while we drive. In the rush and frenzy, food becomes merely a physical sensation.

Through the discipline of pausing and turning our hearts toward God in gratitude before we eat, we elevate eating from an act of mere biology to an occasion for cultivating spiritual life.

Tithing—Habitual Giving

"Bring the whole tithe into the storehouse so that there will be food in My house," says the Lord God (see Mal. 3:8).

My father, Barney McLarty, has been an extravagant giver. One year he gave away more than he made that year. But in addition to his special giving, he has always given 10 percent of his income to the church. One January in the early 1970s he made out a check to "Seventh-day Adventist Church" for $25,000. He put it in an envelope and mailed it to the central office of the Seventh-day Adventist Church in Guatemala. For Dad, it was quite unremarkable. Every year, sometime before April 15, his accountant told him how much he had made the previous year, and he wrote a check for 10 percent of that amount. Sometimes he mailed it to his local church; sometimes he sent it elsewhere.

Tithe is an old word meaning 10 percent. And tithing (devoting 10 percent of one's income to God) is a family tradition Adventists share with many other Christians. It is a spiritual discipline that helps us remember that all we enjoy is a gift from God. It brings to mind the words of Deuteronomy 8:18, "Remember the Lord your God, for it is he who gives you the ability to produce wealth" (NIV). In addition to its effect on our personal spiritual life, tithing also serves as part of the glue that holds our church community together.

Money given to the church and designated "tithe" is pooled and used to pay the clergy and the operating expenses of the church bureaucracy. The range of clergy salaries among Adventists is rather narrow. The senior pastor of the largest Adventist church in North America makes less than twice as much as a pastor in rural Wyoming. This pooling of tithe dollars and restricted variance in salaries helps to foster a strong sense of community. We are all members of one family. (Of course, families also argue about the management of money, and a favorite Adventist debate is the management of tithe money.)

In the Bible, people are directed to use their tithe for a number of purposes. All of them have to do with building community—whether the tithe is being used for a community celebration, the care of the indigent, the support of the clergy, or maintenance of the Temple services (Deut. 14:22-29; Num. 18:26-29; Mal. 3:8-10). It is easy to talk about community, but the way we use our time and spend our money is the real test of our commitment. If we are mature members of the family, we will participate financially. The Adventist practice of tithing is a structured way for members to cooperate in the mission of the church. It is a habit that ties us together as a spiritual family.

Some American Christians protest against the specificity of tithing. They argue that requiring people to give 10 percent is hard-edged legalism inappropriate for people who are free in Christ. I don't find this kind of talk very convincing. If we replace the command and practice of the Hebrew scriptures with the commands given by Jesus in regard to money we will face a far more challenging rule. "Do not store up for yourselves treasures on earth, where moth and rust destroy and where thieves break in and steal. But store up for yourselves treasures in heaven, . . . For where your treasure is, there your heart will be also" (Matt. 6:19-21, NIV).

Taken literally this statement would prohibit savings accounts, mutual funds, stashing money under your mattress, holding stock. It would prohibit the possession of any cash beyond the immediate needs of the moment. This daunting ideal is underlined by the challenge Jesus gave to a young man who came looking for guidance: "Jesus said, 'If you want to be perfect, go, sell whatever you own and give to the poor. This will give you treasure in heaven. Then come and follow me'" (Matt. 19:21).

In light of this directive, the Old Testament rule of 10 percent appears mild, even indulgent. Jesus did not ask every believer to give away everything. In His conversation with the wealthy Nicodemus, for instance, Jesus did not even mention money. Jesus does call us to live as responsible members of the household of God. That necessarily includes participating in the financial life of the family. The 10 percent rule of the Hebrew scriptures is a minimum standard. It is a powerful spiritual discipline that helps us to remember that our money is to be managed for God's glory.

When we devote the first 10 percent of our income to God we are coinvesting with God. It is a way for us to cooperate with God in His mission in the world. God takes our small contribution and makes it an essential part of the vast resources of heaven. God sees to it that our money makes a difference.

In 1996 I was in Oklahoma for camp meeting (the annual convocation of the Seventh-day Adventist Church in the state). A pleasant, gray-haired man introduced himself to me. Mr. Sample said he had a story he thought would be of interest.

In the early 1970s he had been the treasurer of the Seventh-day Adventist Church in Guatemala. There had been a currency devaluation. At that time the church in Guatemala was fairly small and very poor. Most of its budget came from an appropriation from the international church headquarters (called the General Conference). Some time before the devaluation, the regular appropriation had been deposited in a Guatemalan bank. Suddenly, the day after the devaluation, the church had half as much money as it did the day before.

The church leaders met in emergency session to figure out what to do. Obviously, expenses had to be cut—and most of their expenses were in personnel. Pastors were going to have to be laid off. Given the miserable state of the economy, whoever was laid off was really going to struggle financially. They prayed. They agonized. Whom would they cut? What criteria should they use?

Late in the morning, Mr. Sample was called out of the room by his secretary. The day's mail had arrived, and she had a letter for him. It was from Barney McLarty of Memphis, Tennessee, and contained a check for $25,000. Arriving after the devaluation it was worth twice as much in local currency as it would have been a couple days earlier.

The emergency treasury meeting turned into a celebratory prayer meeting. Dr. McLarty's check was sufficient to fill the budget hole created by the devaluation until the next appropriation from the General Conference. No one was laid off.

When Dad wrote the check he had no sense of doing something special. He had friends in Guatemala but knew nothing of the impending currency devaluation. He was just following his lifelong habit of devoting 10 percent of his income to the church. There are many stories of God impressing people to make extraordinary contributions to various persons and ministries. These stories highlight God's ability to communicate with His people. But it's important to honor what God does through our *routine* spiritual disciplines. Habitual giving is no less honored by God than a gift motivated by an extraordinary prompting of the Spirit.

Practicing the habit of giving makes our money available to God for doing special things. It builds the community and shapes our souls in generosity.

Beyond Spiritual Adolescence

So shall we all at last reach unity in the faith and in the knowledge of the Son of God and become fully mature, attaining to the full stature of the fullness of Christ (see Eph. 4:13).

In a normal family, Mother is all-knowing, unfailingly devoted and affectionate, utterly trustworthy, completely able to manage every urgency of our lives. She is the most beautiful person in the world. Then we become teenagers, and that same omnipotent, omniscient woman loses her mind, her manners, her character, and her looks.

As teenagers, we are ruthless in our demands that parents and all other authority figures be flawlessly consistent. (Of course, we cut ourselves considerable slack, but . . .) We scorn the accommodations our parents have made with what they call reality. We secretly or blatantly regard ourselves as truly perspicuous, sage, and competent—quite in contrast to Mom.

Fortunately for most of us, Mother recovers. We're chagrined to discover that we've done a better job of copying our parents' weaknesses than their strengths. While objectively we may be more aware of our parents' real imperfections, as adults we treasure them more than we ever did before.

Adults who remain obsessed with their parents' failings are dangerous or tragic people. They make difficult spouses, prickly friends, and impossible employees. Individuals who fail to grow beyond their adolescent rebellion against their parents never really mature and often pass on their dysfunction to their children.

It's something like that in spiritual life. Whether we first experience the church as children or as adult converts, usually it appears perfect in our eyes. This is God's church. Everything it teaches is true, and all truth that matters is found within its teaching. Its mission is God's mission. God is scarcely capable of acting outside its boundaries.

Time passes. We discover there are flaws and lacunae in the church's theology. Maybe we've been damaged by faulty theology or evil clergy or an incompetent youth leader. We find out Ellen White read and quoted

43

other authors. We read *Spectrum* or *Adventist Today* and learn that scholars in the church question one aspect or another of traditional doctrine. The preacher in our local congregation leaves in moral disgrace. We go through a personal crisis and the "caring church" doesn't exist.

We enter spiritual adolescence. We become engrossed in the failings and hypocrisy of the church. We cannot believe a body that professes to represent Jesus could possibly act with such blatant disregard for the teachings of its Master. We don't understand how anyone with a modicum of intelligence could possibly say with a straight face that they are glad to be part of this church.

This disillusionment is a normal, though painful, part of growing up spiritually. I don't know any way to avoid it. If the church did not appear all-sufficient when we first encountered it, we would never learn enough trust to become wholehearted members. If we never honestly face the church's failings and inadequacies, we will be unable to help our children and friends when they are moving through their own spiritual adolescence. Some measure of disillusionment and identity separation is normal in personal spiritual development. But if we're healthy Christians, we will grow through this adolescence to spiritual adulthood.

As mature believers we move beyond our obsession with the brokenness of the church. We learn to value the church for its strengths and virtues. Instead of scorning the church for its failures, we honor it for its ideals. We acknowledge that, as it is with our parents, so it is with the church—we more faithfully mimic her failings than her strengths.

After adolescence we can no longer naively think the church is perfectly wise or good. We are not toddlers who uncritically regard our spiritual mother as God. But as adults we have grown beyond the juvenile notion that only perfect people can do good or that only perfect organizations are worthy of loyalty and honor. We find new joy in the church. We have fewer illusions, make fewer impossible demands, and move beyond condemnation to affection. We are able to laugh at our own immature rantings and see the real wisdom that is the heritage of the church. Of course, the church is defective. It's made of people like us. But it also preserves and transmits the collective learning of a large group of pilgrims.

New converts and children love the church in its imaginary perfection. Spiritual adolescents despise the church for its real failings. Those who are mature love the church for what it is—the scarred body of Christ, a gathering of broken people such as ourselves, seeking pardon and transformation. A flawed organization pursuing a glorious, impossible dream. A cooperative venture of individuals much worse and much better than average. A mother worthy of honor.*

* This chapter has in mind the ordinary range of function and dysfunction that is characteristic of most families. Since the publication of the first edition of this book, I have received letters from people who have been grievously wounded in the church, especially in the area of sexuality. I do not wish to minimize their pain or the moral responsibility of those who perpetrated or ignored this kind of egregious evil. I do want to challenge those who are trapped in bitterness about the inadequacies and failures of the church of their childhood to move beyond their complaints to healthy maturity.

Steel-belted Radials: the Church as a Tire

A man in your church has his father's wife! And you are proud of it! Shouldn't you rather have been filled with grief and have expelled him from your fellowship? (see 1 Cor. 5:1, 2).

I had not been married long before my wife's brother gave me a quiet lecture on tires. He insisted I put Michelin steel-belted radials on my car. I was going to be driving his sister around, and he wanted her to be safe. He was an expert on all things automotive, and he helped me with my first purchase of good tires. So I listened. It's a good thing.

A few years later, I was driving north on I-15, after a day with my wife's sister, who lived in Fallbrook, California. The kids were asleep in the back seat. My wife was dozing off. I was doing about 70 as I crossed the bridge over I-60.

Then it happened. Right at the joint between the bridge and the regular road surface was an enormous pothole. I didn't see it until the instant before we hit it. Kaboom-boom. The front wheel seemed to take the worst of it. The whole car shuttered. My wife bolted awake, exclaiming, "What happened?" I gripped the steering wheel and held my breath, waiting for the consequences, alert to any aberration in the car's performance. But nothing further happened. Besides the emotional shock my wife and I experienced, there was no indication we had just driven through the mother of all potholes.

Tire engineers constantly tinker with the balance between two competing values: cushion (the softness and suppleness of the tire) and strength (the ability of the tire to withstand bruising encounters with potholes and other assorted road hazards). Both values are absolutely essential.

Rubber gives a tire its cushion and traction. Steel belts provide the strength to withstand abuse as well as hold the high air pressure needed for high performance. It is possible to make all-rubber tires, but they can hold only 15 to 20 pounds of pressure. They're used on swamp buggies that bounce and float their way across boggy land. All-rubber tires would be useless on a Miata or Jeep. They wouldn't have the strength for freeway travel or for the rocks and holes of back roads in the desert. On the other hand, you wouldn't want all-steel tires on your vehicle unless it was a tank or a locomotive.

High-performance tires require a blend of cushion and strength, rubber and steel. Effective spiritual life, both on the individual and corporate levels, requires a corresponding blend of grace and law, tact and toughness, liberty and discipline.

We see this blend in Jesus' ministry. He was wonderfully responsive to the variety of human needs while at the same time exhibiting a steel-strong tenacity of purpose. We find a similar alloy in His teachings. He taught His disciples tact, gentleness, and compassion—a warm responsiveness to human need. And He taught a strict code of conduct, a radical commitment to truth and right doing.

Holy Rubber

We celebrate Jesus for being the very opposite of rigid, legalistic, arbitrary, authoritarian. We celebrate His concern for persons over law, for ministry over mores. He spoke to a Samaritan woman in spite of Jewish proscriptions. He touched a leper in violation of the law. He "broke" the Sabbath to heal a woman who had been ill for 18 years. Jesus adapted Himself to individuals. He didn't have a one-size-fits-all approach. When one man talked with Him about spiritual life, Jesus told him to sell everything he had and give it away. When another wealthy man visited Him, Jesus said nothing about his money and spoke only about his heart ("You must be born again"). Jesus shaped His words and actions for the individual in front of Him. But He was a Man of steel as well.

Holy Steel

The most dramatic example of Jesus' combination of steel and rubber was the day He drove the merchants and currency dealers from the Temple grounds (Matt. 21). Jesus strode through the Temple courtyard swinging a knotted rope, turning over tables, and chasing out the merchants. He terrorized the people accustomed to domination there, demonstrating intimidating steel.

But in the very next sentence after the report of His terrorizing the merchants, we read that Jesus was surrounded by children excitedly singing hosannas, drawn by His warmth and compassion. Steel and rubber. Toughness and tenderness.

The Church

The church must model this same blend of softness and strength, flexibility and unyielding integrity. If we live at either pole, we will be dysfunctional and besmirch the reputation of the Head of the church. I've heard heartbreaking stories of people damaged by excessive or inappropriate church condemnation or rejection—too much steel or bits of steel protruding from the tire. But as culture shifts and we become more tolerant, I hear more frequently about wounds inflicted because the church has failed to confront, rebuke, and repudiate predators with smooth personalities and glib speech who operate in the church. A high-performance church must combine steel and rubber, toughness and tenderness.

Not Enough Steel

Sally was forced by her husband, Bill, to have an abortion. He threatened to divorce her unless she consented. Not long afterward, she discovered that Bill had been seeing a younger woman. Over the next year or so, he flaunted the affair, laughing at Sally's protests and daring her to divorce him. She finally did, and Bill married the "sweet, young thing."

Where was the church in all this? The pastor told Sally to obey her husband and have the abortion because her husband was the head of the family. And when Bill blamed the divorce on Sally, the pastor accepted his statement without verifying it. He agreed to perform the wedding for Bill and his new sweetheart in Bill and Sally's home church.

Bill is still quite active in the church, loves to preach when he gets the opportunity, and is an avid amateur theologian, and the church has been very gracious to his new wife. But is it any wonder that his former wife is no longer a member of the Adventist Church and has serious questions about the justice of God? The church had lots of rubber—for Bill. But it had no steel for Sally. It failed to protect her, to support her, to vindicate her.

The church is called by God to use its influence and authority to champion righteousness, oppose injustice, and protest evil. If a church is going to be a high-performance church, it must be willing to publicly and sternly oppose wickedness such as Bill's.

Once, when I was speaking at a camp meeting, a woman in great distress came to talk. An elder in her church had been arrested for sexual misconduct with a young boy in the church. He was sent to jail for a short time, then released on probation. It was discovered that he'd had other victims in the church over the years. But the church refused to remove him from office because they didn't want to be judgmental!

When a member of the church molests children, the church must sternly and publicly rebuke the molester. It must declare in unequivocal terms: We do not tolerate such behavior. I cannot understand why such a statement is controversial. Grace is not a license to prey.

When someone uses the church as a cover for swindling the elderly, when members are habitually unkind to young people or others in the church, the church as a body must publicly say, "This is not right." The church must protect the vulnerable.

Church discipline is not a rejection of the person; it is not unchristian judging. It is the very spirit of Jesus. It is announcing the judgment of God against oppression and injustice. As the incident with the Temple courtyard merchants demonstrated, Jesus was not wimpy in opposing those who used a religious cover for their unrighteousness.

When pastors are incompetent or derelict and fail to respond appropriately when confronted, they must be removed, not moved. When church administrators lie or use their office for personal gain or fail to appropriately discipline other workers under them, the church must rebuke or remove the administrator.

Paul writes that the church is the pillar and ground of truth (1 Tim. 3:15, KJV). It is the household of God (Eph. 2:19). It is the body of Christ (1 Cor. 12:27). Without discipline, without the resolve to publicly repudiate harmful behavior done by its members and officials, the church makes a mockery of these New Testament ideals.

Tough Enough to Help

A couple asked me to baptize them and I refused. They were living together and planning to get married, but the woman was not yet divorced from her first husband. I insisted she get her marital situation straightened out before I would baptize them. I took heat from one of the elders in my congregation for my judgmentalism.

The couple moved away, but over the next several years they called occasionally from their new city, thanking us for the ministry of our church and telling how they had grown spiritually. Apparently, our toughness built their confidence in our church as a safe place. Our refusal to cooperate in their illicit relationship meant we were cooperating with their consciences even while we refused to cooperate with their choices.

In these kinds of cases, it appears that if I agreed to turn a blind eye to immoral behavior, the participants would experience moral confusion. Deep in their inner core was an ineradicable conviction that what they were doing was wrong. If the church agreed with their choice rather than their deeper, unvoiced conviction, they would not perceive the church as a safe place. They would experience church as a community that could be manipulated, which would mean that it was untrustworthy. When the church courteously but firmly opposes unfaithfulness, it is working to create a healthy community, a safe place.

Hidden Steel

To draw out the tire analogy a little further, if the steel in a tire begins to show, you know there is a problem. A high performance tire must have steel, but it mustn't show. So in church life, if the steel is what is most obvious to others, the church has a problem.

If our young people or visitors or longtime members experience church primarily as a place of steel, we have miserably failed. We earn the right to speak the truth by demonstrating love, "love with skin on it." Real love costs time, sometimes money, and always a sacrifice of our natural desire for our church to look good and make its established members feel right.

Every act of discipline must be wrapped in deep regard for persons and in habits of courtesy and attentiveness. On the other hand, our kindness and permissiveness must be given reliable shape and form by a radical commitment to truth and justice.

Holy Air

To complete the analogy: Tire designers invest brain power and money in the pursuit of the perfect blend of rubber and steel. They ruthlessly test their models and improve them. We should do the same with our patterns of spiritual life, personally and corporately. High-performance Christian living calls for creativity; thorough testing; and sober, clear-sighted analysis. But ultimately, in the world of tires, neither the steel nor the rubber actually carries the car. The best steel-belted radial in the world is useless without something rather intangible—air. The air in the tire is what carries the car.

So with the church. Neither our tact and compassion nor our resolute commitment to righteousness and truth will ultimately enable us to do the job God has assigned us. Those observable human qualities are indispensable but insufficient. It is only as our lives and our congregations are filled with the Spirit of God that we can really achieve the high performance to which we are called.

After we have studied and planned, attended seminars on discipline, friendship evangelism, church growth, and remnant theology, let's give ourselves to prayer, seeking the Holy Spirit. Then when we smash into unexpected potholes, the tire will hold.

Liberals and Conservatives

Let us stop passing judgment on each other. Instead, resolve not to put any stumbling block or obstacle in your brother's way (see Rom. 14:13).

"Master," said John, "we saw a man driving out demons in your name and we tried to stop him because, he is not one of us." "Do not stop him," Jesus said, "for whoever is not against you is for you" (Luke 9:49, 50, NIV).

OK, OK. I know they're tricky labels. And labels often obfuscate as much as clarify. But in this case I can't think of any other convenient shorthand. And while "liberal" and "conservative" are notoriously imprecise, they will work for our present purpose.

Think of the church as a house. The conservatives are the builders; the liberals are the decorators. The builders pour concrete and nail two-by-fours. The decorators add flowers and skylights.

Liberals and conservatives are always arguing over the house. Conservatives think of the house as a fortress against evil. They want it sturdy enough to handle a 9.0 earthquake and an F4 tornado. Conservatives invest huge amounts of time and money in building a strong house and they want it to stay that way. Understandably, they resent anyone messing with it. They fear any change in the structure of the house will make it vulnerable to attack from thieves, termites, tornados, earthquakes, or fire.

Leave it alone, they insist. It's strong. It has served well. Don't fix what ain't broke.

Then liberals come along and start tinkering. They want skylights and larger windows. They insist on carpet in the living room and Italian tile in the kitchen. They want wallpaper in the entry and bedrooms. They want glass blocks in the exterior wall beside the front door to lighten the entry hall. They order new appliances for the kitchen. And while they're at it, they suggest removing the wall between the kitchen and the family room and another wall between the living room and dining room.

Conservatives watch all this remodeling with growing dread. Those openings in the roof for skylights are sure to leak. The larger windows will be extremely vulnerable during hurricanes. And the wallpaper and carpet are just a waste of money.

If conservatives can keep the liberals out of the house, it will be sturdy for sure. Quake proof, wind proof, fire proof. On the other hand, you may end up with a house the kids won't want to live in. Who wants to walk on concrete floors, sleep on cots, and hang blankets over the windows for privacy in the evening?

If the liberals manage to oust the conservatives, we may end up with a gorgeous, comfortable structure that will collapse in a 3.2 quake or blow over in a 50 mph gale. The skylights may leak, the carpets will be beautiful and impossible to clean. The bathroom will be attractive but the plumbing will leak.

In the church, liberals don't build institutions; conservatives do. Colleges, hospitals, publishing houses, summer camps, academies, and churches are all built by conservatives. Conservatives are the people with enough conviction to part with their hard-earned dollars and actually get something going. On the other hand, liberals are the ones flexible enough to bend the original vision to fit the present reality. Liberals are the ones who ask hard questions about efficiency and effectiveness in the light of changes in society.

The Adventist church would have no colleges or medical schools if it weren't for the passionate conviction and drive of conservatives. On the other hand, we would have no colleges sending graduate students to Harvard, Columbia, and Stanford, and no world-class medical school, if it weren't for the liberals in the 1950s who pushed through accreditation.

Conservatives make the best evangelists. They are confident in what they believe. They know what other people need. And their convictions are specific enough to be readily communicated.

Adventist conservatives can point to a church membership in the millions as justification for keeping the house just the way it is. Conservatives have formulated the ideas, gathered the people, and built the institutions that are the targets of liberal remodeling efforts.

But conservatives have children. And when those children grow up, often they need the ministry of liberals. These young people see problems with some aspect or another of their parents' faith or church and are unpersuaded by conventional answers. Their spiritual life is characterized as much by questioning as by conviction. They need more than anything else to know that someone with status in the church hears them, understands them. And if they cannot bring their unruly minds into conformity with every detail of their parents' religion, they need another adult to assure them that this church is still their home. It's OK to live here.

Doubters don't often join self-confident sects, but they are born into them. Homosexuals do not join conservative churches in the same numbers that they grow up in them. Very few geologists or psychiatrists or artists become Adventists. But young people from Adventist homes study geology, psychiatry, and art, and end up with questions that are not readily answered using conventional conservative argument.

You don't have to join the Adventist church if you have troublesome, unanswered questions, but what if you've grown up Adventist? If you treasure the Sabbath and the Great Controversy theme and vegetarianism and life-long friends and several generations worth of institutional loyalty and then find yourself wrestling with geochronology or some other Adventist certainty, to whom do you talk?*

At first you might seek out a convinced, articulate conservative in a bid to revive your old certainties. But if you no longer find conventional answers persuasive and you don't want to move out, then you'll thank God for the ministry of liberals. You will give thanks that someone put in a skylight, took out a wall or two, and put some carpet on the floor.

And if it's your children who are thinking of leaving the church, and their conversations with a liberal keep them in your church, then you'll really give thanks for the decorators. Liberals are the adults in the church whom the children of conservatives can talk to.

This ministry of liberals should recommend itself to conservatives for another reason: When young adults leave the Adventist church because of some specific difficulty, their children are highly unlikely to ever hear the Adventist message. But if questioning young adults remain in the church, their children will have ample opportunity to become acquainted with Adventism and respond for themselves.

Sometimes it happens that the children of a liberal read Ellen White in high school or college and become radical Adventists. These children want a religion that's sturdy and vigorous, that's aggressively evangelistic, that is impatient with human frailty, and bold in its obedience. In other words, they are conservative.

If all Adventists were liberal, sophisticated, and culturally assimilated, where would these "reborn" children of liberals find spiritual mentors? They would have to leave and find a fundamentalist denomination; they would need to go elsewhere to find someone who would affirm their spiritual journey. But since our church includes confident, militant conservatives, the born-again, radical children of liberals can remain at home in the church of their parents. Conservatives are the adults in the church whom children of liberals can admire and with whom they can conspire.

Conservatives don't have high regard for people who don't fit the system. They don't understand the hard questions of their children. They can't see the sincerity that drives honest dissidents to both love the church and argue with it. Liberals have a very hard time with the passionate conviction of young zealots. They don't sympathize with the need for corporate discipline and community norms. Yet the children of the church include both the angst-ridden and the zealous. These children need the respective ministries of liberals and conservatives.

Over the years I've heard people on both the left and right of the church talk as if most of our problems would be solved if we could just get rid of or limit the influence of the "other side." If we could eliminate the corrupting influence of the liberals or the hard edge of the conservatives, then we would have a "just right" church.

I don't believe it. Rather, I am persuaded that, as has been said in other contexts—We ought to stay together for the sake of the children.

---

* This paragraph is addressed to those who have grown up Adventist. The same principle applies to those who are drawn by God to the Adventist community but find themselves not fully persuaded on every detail of doctrine.

A Park in Time

Remember the Sabbath day to keep it holy. Six days you are to labor and do all your work, but the seventh day is the Sabbath of the Lord your God (see Ex. 20:8).

I remember Overton Park in Memphis as a magical place. On Sabbath afternoons my parents took us there for walks in the forest of old growth oaks and hickories. We looked for crawdads in the creek and fed the ducks in the lake. Summer evenings we enjoyed concerts at the band shell. I remember flying kites there, swinging on the swings, and eating watermelon. There was an art academy set in a sweep of lawn, and on the park's north side, the zoo. For a city kid, there was no better place in the world than Overton Park.

I remember one other aspect of life in Memphis in the 1950s and early 1960s. It took forever to go anywhere. There were no freeways. When the first section of freeway opened to traffic, it was one of the seven wonders of the world—four lanes wide and no traffic lights. Riding on it seemed like flying.

The master plan called for a beltway around town and a cross-town expressway as part of Interstate 40. The beltway was the easier right-of-way to acquire. The east-west route through the established neighborhoods in the heart of the city progressed more slowly. The greatest challenge was finding a way through or around a stretch of grand homes that ran north and south through the center of town—right across the projected path of the cross-town expressway. (In Memphis, as in most places, you did not bulldoze the homes of the wealthy.) There was one obvious gap in this roadblock of fine homes: Overton Park. Fortunately for the planners, while there were exclusive neighborhoods north and south of the park, on both the east and west sides there were working class neighborhoods that would present little effective opposition to an expressway.

There was just one problem. An elderly woman with a lot of money didn't want the park desecrated by an expressway. And she went to court.

Nearly everyone I knew was outraged by this woman's opposition to this road going through the park. Memphis desperately needed an expressway. And the park route was the most obvious, least expensive, and most politically feasible. Figuring it was just a matter of time before common sense prevailed, the state moved ahead with construction. They built the freeway to within a couple of miles of the park on the east, and purchased the right-of-way and demolished houses right up to the park border.

The court battles dragged on for 20 years. The park won. There is a gap in the interstate in the middle of Memphis. Interstate 40 is routed around Memphis on the northern beltway. Most of those who, 30 years ago, thought the old woman was crazy, now realize the wisdom of her opposition to cutting up the park with an expressway. When they take their grandkids to the zoo, they're glad it's not bordered by a thundering highway. It's good that the view north from the art academy does not feature fences, exit signs, and passing semi-trailers. And it's right that when you golf or take your kids for a walk in the woods, you hear birds, not traffic.

Memphis still needs a cross-town expressway, but the city would be immeasurably poorer if it had allowed an expressway to cut through the heart of Overton Park.

The idea of using the park's open space to improve the transportation infrastructure of Memphis was rooted in historical precedent. When the city wanted to build an art academy, it was cheaper to site it in the park than to buy more land. And art seemed to fit the purpose of the park. The park had long housed the zoo. And the animals seemed an appropriate accompaniment to the woods and ponds already there. Then there was the fire station. The wealthy homeowners in the area had insisted on better fire coverage, and they were not about to sacrifice one of their fine homes. No one would miss half an acre of woods. So the city sited the fire station in the southwest corner of the park. If it hadn't been for the elderly woman and her lawyers, pragmatists would have bisected the park with an expressway.

Open space in a city must be fiercely defended or it will be used for "more productive" purposes. Without champions to stop it, the press of development will occupy every square inch, leaving the city terribly impoverished.

Sabbath is like a park in time. It is intended by God as a tranquil open space in the frenzy of our lives. But like open space in a city, without constant vigilance it will disappear. Adventists believe we have been called to act as guardians of this park in time.

The idea of a weekly holy day (whether Sabbath or Sunday) has disappeared from American society. In the year 2000 in Seattle, Boeing proposed a floating work week in which work on the weekend would be treated like any other day of the week. Any set of five days would be paid as a regular work week—Monday to Friday or Wednesday to Sunday or Friday to Tuesday. It would all be the same. No more time-and-a-half for work on Saturday or Sunday.

In most Christian churches, Sunday is regarded as a convenient day for church attendance, but not as a holy day. Among American Protestants, there are a few voices lamenting the loss of the Sabbath (Sunday.) And the head of the Roman Catholic Church recently issued a strong statement about the sacredness of Sunday. But these are isolated voices in a larger cultural trend to fill up every available hour with "productive" busyness.

Nearly every adult I know needs more time—more time for work, business, education, shopping, and home and auto maintenance. We don't have enough time for a Sabbath, whether it is Saturday or Sunday. The Sabbath needs a champion as much as Overton Park did.

It would be silly to argue that a park is the most important need of the city. Does a city need parks more than roads, a water system, courts, or fire stations? The city needs all of this and more. And it would be silly to argue Sabbath is the most important need of modern life or the modern church. But while Sabbath is not *most important*, it is a vital constituent of Christian spiritual life.

Parks require community protection. We make rules: No freeways. No fire stations. No Taco Bell. No dogs off leash. No wood gathering. Of course, every rule has exceptions. The park sign reads, "No flower gathering," but who will complain if a child picks a dandelion bouquet? We would oppose the construction of a McDonald's but welcome the services of an ice cream cart on the 4th of July. An expressway would destroy the park, but paved roads make it easier for families to gather in the picnic grounds.

There are Sabbath rules: No work. No hockey matches. No changing the oil in my car. No house painting. No TV news. No hiring others to work for me. To generalize and modernize the Sabbath commandment: On Sabbath quit your struggle to secure your place in the world. Instead, rest in the security God offers. Stop your struggle to make money, earn grades, win the championship, beautify your home, or fix your car. All these things are necessary. You have six days to do them. On Sabbath ignore your failures and inadequacies and achievements and successes and give attention to God's accomplishments and promises. And remember, the Sabbath is not just for you but for all whose lives and work are under your direction.

Fixed boundaries and consistent enforcement are a necessary condition for the preservation of the special nature of a park. It's the same with the

Sabbath. The only way for us to enjoy its blessings is for us to embrace the firm boundaries set in Scripture. If God gave us permission to merely take some time off, most of us would say thank you, then explain that we are just too overcommitted right now to take any time off. So God commanded us to take the time off. He ordered us to stop our important tasks and take 24 hours for fellowship with Him and with our families.

The frenzied pace of our culture is pressuring us to build multiple freeways through the few open spaces left in our lives. The requirements of commerce and personal achievement threaten to completely dominate the human landscape. Don't let it happen in your life. Keep the freeway out of the park, and not just for yourself. Our resolve in park-tending will insure that the woods, zoo, duck pond, and picnic tables—and the surrounding tranquility—remain available for our children, grandchildren, and neighbors. Our Sabbathkeeping is a bold vote for the preservation of a priceless sanctuary, an irreplaceable park in time, for generations to come.

A Magnificent Emptiness

A great and powerful wind tore the mountains . . . but the Lord was not in the wind. After the wind there was an earthquake, but the Lord was not in the earthquake. After the earthquake came a fire, but the Lord was not in the fire. And after fire came a still, small voice. When Elijah heard it, he pulled his cloak over his face and went out and stood at the mouth of the cave (see 1 Kings 19:11-13).

It wasn't exactly kidnapping, but I was being transported against my will in the back seat of a blue Datsun. In the front seat were two women, Mina and Teresa. All of us were students at Pacific Union College in northern California.

It was spring break. The women and I had delivered a truckload of donated clothing, furniture, and household appliances to Holbrook Indian Mission School in Arizona. Now we were headed back to college, but Mina had this bee in her bonnet about seeing the Grand Canyon. I protested that it was too far out of the way. I was in a hurry to get back to school, and the side trip from Flagstaff up to the canyon would add hours to the trip. Besides, I knew we were in for a disappointment. Sure, I had seen the pictures. I had heard the stories. But I didn't see how any hole in the ground could ever live up to the kind of hype associated with the Grand Canyon. But what could I say? The car belonged to Mina. We headed for the Grand Canyon.

At Flagstaff we turned off Interstate 40 and drove north. I buried myself in a book, probably something exciting such as epistemology in the theology of the Eastern Orthodox Church. Occasionally I'd sneak a glance out the window. What I saw confirmed my suspicions. Pine trees. An endless blur of trunks and needles.

I looked up again when we stopped at the entrance. Still nothing worth seeing. Finally we pulled into the parking lot. Mina and Teresa got out. I stayed in the backseat, staring at my book, refusing to get sucked into this silly excursion.

But after a couple of minutes I thought, *Well, since I'm here I may as well take a look.* Closing the book, I climbed out of the backseat and ambled across the parking lot toward the canyon.

As I walked up to the edge of the canyon my mouth dropped open. I sat down on a rock and just stared, dumbstruck with wonder and awe. I forgot everything I had ever read about the canyon. I forgot all the pictures I'd seen. I forgot everything anyone had ever told me. I was utterly enthralled and enchanted. I didn't move until Mina tapped me on the shoulder half an hour later. "It's time to go." I reluctantly returned to the car, promising myself, *I'm coming back.*

Sabbath is like the Grand Canyon. The Grand Canyon is a park in space. Its boundaries can be drawn on a map or traced over the landscape. Sabbath is a park in time. Its boundaries are drawn on a calendar or traced in our weeks.

On my second visit to the canyon, I hiked 3,000 feet down to Indian Gardens and then out to Plateau Point. This point is on the edge of the inner gorge, which drops another 2,000 feet straight down to the Colorado River.

For a couple of hours I just sat there, taking in the grandeur. I kept trying to get my mind around the reality that the great walls surrounding me were not really mountains but were, in fact, the sides of the ditch I was sitting in.

I have read eloquent literature about the canyon. I've stared enchanted at photographs and paintings. But there is no way to capture with words or film or paint the canyon's grandeur and immensity. You have to experience it. In all that immensity there is an extraordinary sense of the presence and power of God.

The Sabbath is something like that. No matter how much you hear about the Sabbath, no matter how many words you read about it, there's no real understanding of its wonder and value apart from direct experience.

Another intriguing parallel between Grand Canyon National Park and the Sabbath is that both are much easier to define by using negative statements than positive ones.

What is Grand Canyon National Park? First of all, as a park it's a place where routine commercial and civic activity is excluded. You can't find a mall. There are no condominiums lining the river at the bottom of the canyon. And the rim of Tonto Plateau isn't lined with bed and breakfasts offering gourmet meals, distinctive rooms, and fantastic views. There's no hospital, no auto repair shops, no Taco Bell or Burger King. No city hall.

There are some services available in Grand Canyon Village on the South Rim, but for the most part, routine civic and commercial activities are excluded.

Notice: It's not bad stuff that's excluded. Condos and houses, malls and grocery stores, car dealerships and hospitals, landfills and freeways are indispensable components of our society. They are essential for "the good life" that most of us appreciate. But we exclude these good things from our parks in order to make room for something better—something that gets crowded out in the press of everyday, routine business and government—an extraordinary awareness of the presence and grace of God.

Just as a park is defined in negative terms, so is the Sabbath: "Remember the Sabbath day, to keep it holy. Six days you shall labor and do all your work, but the seventh day is the Sabbath of the Lord your God. In it you shall do no work: you, nor your son, nor your daughter, nor your male servant, nor your female servant, nor your cattle, nor your stranger who is within your gates. For in six days the Lord made the heavens and the earth, the sea, and all that is in them, and rested the seventh day. Therefore the Lord blessed the Sabbath day and hallowed it" (Ex. 20:8-11, NKJV).

Notice how much of this Sabbath commandment is expressed negatively. Don't work. Don't have your children or servants or animals work. Don't. Don't. Don't. And it's the same with a park. Don't litter. Don't cut across switchbacks. No fires outside the campground grates. No dogs on trails. No off-road driving. The exclusions are the necessary condition for experiencing the wonder and rapture of the park. The Golden Arches would not improve the view from the South Rim. A network of roads and bridges crisscrossing the canyon would not make it more grand. And if dirt bikes and ATVs zoomed up and down the trails, a hiker would not have the same sense of God's accompanying presence when he or she ventured down the South Kaibab Trail.

Grand Canyon National Park takes this notion of negative definition further than other parks. If you go to Yellowstone National Park, what you notice are things such as geysers and elk and bison. What makes the park special is what's there. If you go to Smoky Mountain National Park you notice the mountains. But what makes the Grand Canyon special is precisely what's not there. The physical reality that seizes your eyes and enchants your heart is created by the absence of cubic miles of rock and dirt. The Grand Canyon is a magnificent emptiness.

Sabbath, too, is a magnificent emptiness. The most obvious feature of Sabbath is what is missing—all the busyness and demands of ordinary life. The deadlines and pressures of earning a living, maintaining a house, keeping up the yard, or fixing your car. Sabbathkeepers often speak of the spiritual and social blessings they experience on the Sabbath, but what is noticeable to on-lookers, to non-Sabbathkeeping observers, is what is missing. They notice what we don't do.

The commercial and scholastic emptiness of Sabbath is filled with a sweet sense of the presence of God. The commandment drains cubic miles of pressure, obligation, and frenzy from our Sabbaths, creating a sacred space that restores and soothes. Of course, God is present everywhere and all the time. God is not limited to the Sabbath. But Sabbath, by liberating us from the demands and pressures of ordinary life, offers us opportunity for extraordinary fellowship with our Savior and Creator. It is, indeed, a magnificent emptiness.

God's Wedding Ring

I gave them the Sabbath—a day of rest every seventh day—as a symbol between them and me, to remind them that it is I, the Lord, who sanctifies them, that they are truly my people (see Eze. 20:12).

It's a gorgeous spring day. Warm sun paints the patio where Janet is planting petunias and snapdragons in large terra cotta pots. After pressing the soil around the last petunia in the current pot, she pulls her hands from the dirt, pushes back her hair with the back of her hand, then studies her fingers. She rubs the dirt off her wedding ring.   The dull gleam of gold on her finger takes her back to the day she first met Andrew.

She was waiting tables at a cheap Italian restaurant on First Avenue, a block from Bellevue Hospital. It wasn't the job she'd dreamed of when she left Shaker Heights after her junior year in college. She was going to be an actress. She knew it would be hard, but she had some secretarial skills and figured she could make enough to live on while she developed her acting career. But all she could find was temp work, and too often she didn't even get that. She met a guy at an audition. They dated a few times. When she didn't have the money for another week at the YMCA, she didn't dare call home for help. She moved in with him.

They'd been living together three months the first time he hit her. He was terribly apologetic. Promised it would never happen again. But it did. Usually when money was tight. So, she'd taken the job waiting tables at Pappa Roma's. It didn't pay much, but it was regular, and sometimes the tips were good.

One night her boyfriend came home drunk. Again. They got into a shouting match, and before she knew it, he was hitting her. Again. He ended up sobbing that he was sorry. She slept cuddled in his arms. He hadn't broken anything and in the morning she was able to crawl out of bed. She did what she could with makeup to hide the bruises and headed for Roma's.

At lunch time, Roma's was always packed. Doctors and staff from the hospital. Relatives of patients. Andrew had come in with a couple of interns for lunch. Janet bantered with them a bit, angling for a tip. OK, she flirted. She needed the money.

The doctors got up to leave, but instead of heading out the door, Andrew came back to the kitchen looking for her.

"Are you all right?" he asked.

"Sure. Never felt better." She tried to be flippant.

"Look," he said, "I'm an ER doc. You did a pretty good job with your makeup, but I do know a battered face when I see one. I'm worried about you. I don't want to see you down the street where I do my business. I much prefer seeing you here. So take care of yourself, OK? You don't have to let anyone beat you up. Get some help before you get killed, OK?"

And then he was gone.

Turned out Andrew was in his final year of an emergency room residency. He was single. He kept coming to Roma's for lunch.

Janet still can't quite figure out how it happened. But they've been married 12 years now. What had he seen in her? What had he seen behind the makeup on someone else's battered girlfriend?

With Andrew's encouragement and financial support she'd gone back to college and earned a fine arts degree. His family, an old, established Connecticut family, had embraced her as one of their own. Their three children were a delight. Her husband's practice was going well.

She is wealthy, socially secure and spiritually whole—all because of her husband's love. And every time she glances at her hand and sees that wedding ring, she remembers.

Sabbath is God's wedding ring. It's a reminder of His surprising pursuit of our love, a symbol of our privileges as the chosen people of God, a declaration to the world of our admiration for our Heavenly Husband.

"I gave them the Sabbath—a day of rest every seventh day—as a symbol between them and me, to remind them that it is I, the Lord, who sanctifies them, that they are truly my people." "Hallow my Sabbaths; for they are a symbol of the contract between us to help you remember that I am the Lord your God" (Eze. 20:12, 20, TLB).

The word sanctify means to set apart. God sanctifies His people; He sets them apart for a special relationship with Himself. He gives us the Sabbath to help keep alive our awareness of His love in a world full of evidence to the contrary. The Sabbath reminds us of where we have come from and what God has in mind for us.

Sabbath celebrates God's initiative and God's intentions in His relationship with humans. None of us complain if our beloved is good looking, wealthy, smart, caring, and responsive. But the Bible pictures God coming and wooing us while we were broken and poor. He found us when we were living with a violent boyfriend, waiting tables in a cheap restaurant. It mattered to Him that we were getting beaten up. He saw in us a beauty no mirror could reflect. He won our hearts and made us His own. The Sabbath symbolizes all that.

"We love him, because he first loved us" (1 John 4:19, KJV).

When the kindness and love of God our Savior appeared, he saved us—not by works of righteousness which we have done, but according to his mercy (see Titus 3:4, 5).

"And you shall call His name Jesus, for He will save His people from their sins" (Matt.1:21, NKJV).

These Bible verses voice one of the central spiritual messages of the Sabbath: God wants us. God takes pleasure in saving us.

Is Sabbath Arbitrary or Personal?

At first thought, the Sabbath seems rather arbitrary. Why the seventh day? The year, month, and day are based on readily-observable natural rhythms. But what's the week based on? In spite of significant scholarly efforts to find an ordinary historical origin for the seven-day week, the best evidence continues to be that it originated in the Jewish practice of keeping Sabbath. And the Jews kept Sabbath because God said, "On the seventh day rest!" Society has its week and believers have their Sabbath because of the arbitrary command of God: Take the seventh day off.

I used the word arbitrary deliberately, to be provocative. A much better word is personal. The Sabbath is a personally-chosen gift of time from God to His people. Part of its charm is in its personal—you could almost say, in its idiosyncratic—nature. Like Janet's ring.

Janet could go to a jeweler and buy a replacement ring. It would give her the appearance of being married and might even be prettier than the original ring. But no ring she bought could ever convey to her the same message of affection and love that her husband's ring does. He chose and won her, and he chose and purchased the ring. Only he could give her an adequate replacement ring that would speak of the same personal (arbitrary) choice of her as his bride.

It's the same with the Sabbath. There's nothing intrinsically unique about Sabbath time. It's like every other day, except for the personal intention and action of God. Taking one day off every week, no matter which day it is, provides many of the benefits of the real Sabbath. Any day off could provide release from ordinary work and the crushing stress so many of us work under. Any commonly accepted day could provide us with an opportunity for corporate worship. Any day is better than no day.

But no substitute sabbath can ever convey the personal message of divine affection embedded in the Sabbath. This is the primary argument against substituting Sunday for Saturday as the Sabbath. Sunday can appropriately commemorate Jesus' resurrection, and it offers a convenient time for church services. But it does not have the overtones of divine provision that the Bible links with Sabbath. Sunday observance is a gift from Christians to God, but as a replacement for the divine gift of Sabbath it borders on the sacrilegious.

Sabbath is God's wedding ring, a reminder of where God has brought us from, a symbol of His abiding affection, a promise of an eternal future together. It is one of the great treasures of Adventism. It is too precious to keep to ourselves.

A Good and Welcome Legalism

"Oh, how I love your law! I meditate on it all day long. . . . I have more insight than all my teachers, for I meditate on your statutes" (Ps.119:97-99, NIV).

A deep appreciation for law has been a hallmark of Adventist thinking since the earliest days of our movement. While at times Adventist concern for law has been an unhealthy obsession, a high regard for law remains one of the treasures of Adventist spirituality.

If you are acquainted with the people of Latin America, Africa, or the Middle East, you know the citizens of these societies are every bit as generous, noble, and virtuous as individuals in the United States. Maybe more so. But political, legal, and commercial life across much of these regions is tragically dysfunctional, and much of this dysfunction has to do with their weak legal systems. In these societies, personal relationship is everything. When the law offers no check on the use of position for personal advantage and no leverage for individuals without connections and power, all of life is degraded. Against this backdrop the relative strength of American law and the courts is seen to be a good and welcome legalism.

But it isn't just in civic and commercial life that a high regard for law promotes healthy function. A satisfying spiritual life is dependent on the order and reliability associated with law. And human sexual attraction, which offers the most wonderful sense of connection and intimacy, separated from the constraints of law frequently becomes dysfunctional and even abusive.

What is Law?

Law as I'm using it here includes the Ten Commandments, of course. And Adventists are famous for the emphasis we have placed on them—reflecting both their unique prominence in the Bible and our concern for the Sabbath commandment, which is the most public marker of our community. But *law* also includes the commands to love God, to forgive one another, and to believe on Jesus. Often, when Adventists speak of "the law" they are referring to the fundamental notion of right and wrong. Law is shorthand for duty and obligation. It is what others expect; it is what God requires; ultimately it is what is congruent with the moral field of the universe.

A major theme in Adventist theology among both liberals and conservatives is the notion that moral law is analogous to natural law. Moral law is not merely arbitrary statements by God or by prophets about what people ought to do. Rather, moral law is a description of the fundamental spiritual structure of the universe. Evil actions naturally have deadly consequences. Noble actions naturally exude life-giving influences. Law is not arbitrary or changeable. This approach balances the role of law as imperative (a statement of what we ought to do) and descriptive (a statement of how things work).

In this large sense, the Bible or the Ten Commandments are not themselves "the law"; rather, they bear witness to the law. I take this to be the meaning of Jesus' statement that all the Law and the Prophets hang on the two commandments of love (Matt. 22:40). Alden Thompson has written about "The One, The Two, and The Ten," in an effort to help us understand the inner coherence of Scripture. The core principle of love is elaborated first to the two commands—Love God with your entire being and your neighbor as yourself. Then to the Ten Commandments. Then beyond that to the numerous specific divine directives given in all kinds of settings and recorded by the Bible writers.

Understood in this broad sense, law is absolutely indispensable for spiritual, social, and civic health. Nearly every human interaction is touched by law. Law is so much a part of us that we are usually unaware of its presence. As we move from basic principles to rules, the rules have to be specific enough that we can understand how they apply to the concrete realities of our particular life. On the other hand, if the rules are going to inspire obedience, they need to be based on principles that are widely embraced.

Every area of life has its laws. The apostle Paul, in arguing against soul-deadening legalism, writes of "the law of the Spirit of life," indicating that even the most vibrant and free spiritual life is characterized by the order and harmony of law.

Law and God

Some people have an instinctive, deep confidence in God. "God said it. I believe it. That settles it." Their faith is simple and untroubled. But for many, the question Can God be trusted? is intensely problematic. Is

God good? Is God fair? One of the major projects of Adventist theology has been to address these questions.

Adventists believe that law in its most fundamental form is not an arbitrary imposition of rules by God upon humans; rather, law is a description of the habits of God, or in the language of Ellen White, "Law is the transcript of [God's] character" (God's Amazing Grace, p. 141).

God is not right merely because He says so. God is right because there is an absolute congruence between what He requires and what He is/does. The very structure of the universe is a reflection of God. Our inescapable human sense of right and wrong is a reflection of God. God Himself operates within boundaries, within limits. God must do right. Not simply in the sense that if God does it, it is right, but in the sense of holding Himself to the norms that He expressed in Creation and that govern our best thoughts and sensibilities.

One stream of Christian theology argues that human questions about divine justice are simply irrelevant. If God calls something right, it is right just because God said so. There is no objective, universal criteria by which the Creator can be evaluated. Adventists, on the other hand, believe that the Bible shows that human questions do matter. Every human question about justice and fairness will be dealt with before history is finished and we enter the eternity of bliss. Law may be a divine creation, but having created it, God Himself is defined in part by law and will not violate it.

The Bones of Beauty

I collect bones. Over the years I've picked up the skulls of deer, elk, a bobcat, a beaver, mice, and rats. I've collected ribs, vertebra, pelvises, phalanges, and leg bones. I'm fascinated by the massive strength of an elk femur and the tiny grace of a mouse tibia. Bones are beautiful. But their beauty pales in comparison to the loveliness and grace of the body forms they support.

I was talking with a friend after church. In the far corner of the parking lot, a couple of teenagers whom I knew were talking. He had a nice car and she was sitting on the front fender. There was evident chemistry between them, and I wondered if I was observing a casual conversation or a budding romance. I had a hard time keeping my eyes on my own conversation, and I noticed that my friend was having a hard time, too. The truth is, neither of us was looking at the car or the guy. Our problem was that the young woman he was talking to had very long legs. And she was wearing a very short skirt. That combination was working its very predictable magic.

For all my documented interest in skeletons, no one would believe that I was glancing across the parking lot because of that young woman's tibia, fibula, patella, and femur. But while I was not really looking at bones, the enchanting beauty that drew my eyes was utterly dependent on the strength and rigidity of a healthy skeleton. Humans possess neither beauty nor health apart from a sturdy skeleton.

In contrast, I remember early in my ministry meeting a young woman named Gloria. She had a magical laugh. She was bright and funny—but nothing to look at. Her sister was a tall, slender five feet ten. Gloria was a lumpy, dumpy four feet eight. She moved around in her Brooklyn apartment with crutches. When she left the house she traveled by wheelchair. If you did not hear her voice or watch her eyes you would find nothing attractive about her. What was her problem? Brittle bone disease, she called it. Osteogenesis imperfecta. In this syndrome, bones have little strength. They break under very little pressure. Sufferers of most types of this disease do not live long. You have to have strong bones for health and beauty.

Law serves as the skeleton in spiritual life. We like stories about spiritual life that feature ecstasy, wonder, and miracles. But most people do not find their lives characterized by frequent miracles or continuous rapture. At times God seems distant, the Bible appears uninteresting or untrue, and faith feels like fantasy. In these spiritual "dry times," the skeleton of habits and religious practices becomes obviously indispensable.

We do not argue that law and duty are more important than sweetness and faith. That would be silly. No one falls in love with a skeleton. Spiritual disciplines must not be the essence of our spiritual life. The purpose of the skeleton is to support the life and beauty of the body. The role of duty and obligation, of spiritual disciplines, is to provide a sturdy framework of support for faith, hope, and love.

A friend of mine once argued that genuine Christianity knows nothing of duty. A follower of Jesus should never do something just because he or she is supposed to. Instead, authentic Christians do only those things that arise from within as spontaneous and glad impulses.

But then, he was not a parent. Changing heavy diapers, cleaning up vomit from some little person's bed at 3:30 a.m., or saying No to a teenager's tearful demands does not feel like "a spontaneous and glad impulse." These are loving actions. They correspond to our deepest desires to do our children good. But sometimes we do them only because they are the right thing to do, not because we feel like it at the moment. When we think of love, the first thing that comes to mind is not years of attending our beloved as she battles cancer or as he descends slowly into the nightmare of Alzheimer's. We don't think of the terribly difficult, almost impossibly painful, work of rebuilding a marriage after an affair. But these things are every bit as much love as kisses and birthday parties, flowers and bedtime stories.

At some point in married life, nearly everyone encounters someone who seems more desirable than his or her spouse. Sometimes it is only the stern word of the law, "Thou shalt not commit adultery," that saves the marriage. Obviously a marriage that is only duty and obligation is far less than God's ideal. God's purpose for husbands and wives is that they will experience a union that reflects the very union of the Trinity (Gen. 2:24). But a 50-year-old marriage rich in affection and shared history never happens if couples do not allow law to keep them during times of strain or illicit attraction. Law cannot create love or build rich, intimate relationships. But law builds the fence that protects the garden of love from the assaults of competing lovers, restless hormones, boredom, or exhaustion. Law is a friend of love. Truly beautiful love requires the skeleton of commitment and the habits of caring.

The Rope of Grace

Great peace have they who love your law, and nothing can make them stumble (see Ps. 119:165).

I grew up in Memphis, Tennessee, a city full of trees. From my earliest days I climbed. And when life finally brought me close to rocky cliffs, I was immediately addicted. Even now, when I walk near a boulder or rock face I get the itch to climb. I can feel it in my fingers. They want to feel for handholds, for finger holds. They are hungry for the rough texture and solidity of the rock. But curiously, for all my love of rock climbing, my most vivid memories of clambering about on rock are of moments of terror.

In grade school, my closest friend was my cousin Rick. His mother was my favorite aunt. She invited me to accompany them on a summer trip from our home in Memphis to California. I was thrilled.

We spent a few days at a cabin in Forest Falls in the mountains above San Bernardino, California. In our explorations, Rick and I naturally were drawn to the cliffs and rock faces around the falls. I remember climbing out along a ledge above the falls, my back to the cliff as I inched along, gazing down at the plunge pool at the base of the falls.

Then it happened. I leaned too far forward. Staring down at the leaping, splashing spray, I lost my balance. I could feel myself falling. And there was nothing I could do. I couldn't catch myself by putting my foot forward—there was nothing but empty space. And there was nothing behind me to grab on to.

I can still remember the first thought that went through my mind: *This is really going to mess up Aunt Velma's vacation!*

Then I felt a presence, a pressure, pushing me back against the cliff. I didn't fall.

After I started breathing again, I inched my way back off the ledge to safer ground. And I promised myself I'd never get into a predicament like that again.

But it was a promise impossible to keep. The addiction to climbing

72

was too strong. I remember climbing cliffs along the Big Sur with my brothers. I have vivid memories of working my way along a rocky spine in southern France with three friends from seminary. In each instance, what is most vivid in my recollections is the terror of nearly falling.

I got married and still climbed, but when our first child was born, I quit. My daughter needed a father. And the kind of climbing I did was risky. It's called free solo. Just the rock and I. My fingers and toes and elbows and fists against gravity. If I fall, I fall.

But there was one more time. It happened in Ohio, of all places. Near Dayton there is a gorge in a state park, with walls 20 to 30 feet high. As my wife and I were walking through the gorge, we came across a group of people climbing a wall.

We sat on a park bench to watch. And I felt the old itch. The wall didn't look that difficult. There was a nice crack that ran all the way to the top. We hadn't watched long when the instructor of the group turned to a bystander and asked, "Would you like to try?"

The fellow said, "Sure."

At that point I knew I was going to stay there until they left or I climbed. It appeared this was not a closed group.

The newcomer came over and the instructor started him up the wall. "Put your right foot here. Put your right hand there and your left hand there. Now pull yourself up and put your left foot there. Now move your right hand over to that crack." The instructor continued calling directions and suggestions as the fellow inched up the cliff.

Then it happened. Five feet from the top, the novice climber was reaching for a handhold when his toe slipped and he fell.

He fell only six inches because before the instructor allowed him to put one finger on the rock, he put a safety harness on him. The harness was attached to a rope that went up and passed through a couple of carabiners attached to webbing anchored to a large tree, then back down to the instructor's hands (an arrangement known to climbers as a top belay). As that fellow climbed, the instructor carefully reeled in the slack, keeping the rope somewhat taut all the way up.

So when the man couldn't hold himself on the rock, he fell no more than six inches before the rope caught him. He dangled for a few seconds like a spider on a thread, then got his toes and fingers back on the rock and continued climbing until he reached the top.

This story reminds me of Paul's words in Ephesians 2:8, 9: "For it is by grace you have been saved, through faith—and this not from yourselves, it is the gift of God—not by works, so that no one can boast" (NIV).

There is only one source of security for the Christian: God's grace. It is the rope of grace. But the New Testament is equally emphatic that Christians are expected to climb, to pursue holiness. Jesus urges us to attempt the most amazing feats, to be perfect as our Father in heaven is perfect (Matt. 5:48).

Peter writes: "Make every effort to add to your faith goodness; and to goodness, knowledge; and to knowledge, self-control; and to self-control, perseverance; and to perseverance, godliness; and to godliness, brotherly kindness; and to brotherly kindness, love" (2 Peter 1:5-7, NIV).

Sounds like that climbing instructor. "Put your right hand there. Grab that knob with your left hand. Put your right toe here. Now, pull up and plant your left foot there. Now move your right hand over . . . "

Jesus wants us to move up the wall. He wants us to pursue moral and spiritual excellence. In the Sermon on the Mount He challenged His disciples: "You have heard that it was written do not kill. I tell you do not hate. You have heard that it was written do not commit adultery. I tell you don't even allow yourself to lust. Be merciful even as your Father in heaven is merciful" (see Matt. 5 and Luke 6).

Jesus had high expectations for His disciples. He expected them to climb, to live godly and holy lives in an ungodly, sinful social context. But—and this is crucial to understanding the Christian life—before He set them climbing, He first secured them with the top belay of His grace.

All the time that other fellow was climbing, I was sitting there watching, hoping. Would they invite me to climb? I watched them lower the other man to the ground. Then the instructor turned and asked if I wanted to climb.

I jumped up with embarrassing eagerness and walked over to the base of the wall. The instructor handed me the harness and I promptly starting putting it on upside down. He corrected me, then closely supervised the rest of my outfitting. He carefully tied me into the line with a figure-eight knot and checked all the straps and fasteners on the harness. Finally he started me up the cliff.

"Put your right foot here. Put your right hand there and your left hand there. Now, pull yourself up and put your left foot there. Now move your right hand over . . . "

He started to say more but didn't. I was climbing faster than he could call out the moves. As I moved up the cliff I could hear conversation from the ground. "Yea, sure he was a beginner. Uh huh. Yea, right." I was climbing well. I could feel it. I could tell the watchers were impressed.

I reached the top, turned around and sat on the edge. "Now what should I do?"

"We can lower you on the rope or you can climb down."

"What I'd like to do," I said, "is to climb down over that way." I pointed off to the side, to a route I had watched the instructor try to climb earlier. It's always easier to climb up than to climb down—I was asking to climb down the route the instructor hadn't been able to climb up.

"Go ahead," he called.

I started down. Again I could hear the comments. I was climbing better than I'd ever climbed in my life. Then I reached a tough spot. The cliff bulged out, then in. I began working my way around this bulge, desperately searching the wall for toeholds and finger holds. At one point I called out, "I think I'm going to fall."

"That's all right," the instructor called back, "I've got you."

At that moment I remembered all those other times I thought I was going to fall. They had always been moments of terror. I worried about ruining Aunt Velma's vacation or the summer trip for a group of my friends. I battled sheer, crippling terror. And my climbing ability would be diminished by all the energy being consumed by my fear and worry.

This time, however, I laughed, then focused all my energies on gluing myself to the rock. I spread my fingers. Gripped with my toes. Clinched my fist in a crack. Wedged with my elbow.

And made it past the bulge. A few more moves and I was down. To applause.

What made the difference? Why was I able to climb at the very edge of my ability and beyond? Because this time I was secured by the rope. When I said, "I'm going to fall," the instructor calmly assured me, "Don't worry. I've got you." I was free to climb because my security, my safety, had nothing to do with my climbing ability. My security was in the rope that ran through the instructor's hands.

In fact, I was no more or less safe than the bungling novice who fell off on his way up. I was no more secure than a person who couldn't climb past the first foothold. For all the people who climbed on that wall that afternoon, their security was in the rope and the hands that held it.

And that's the way it is for us spiritually. Our security, our safety, is not rooted in our moral or spiritual strength, in our ability to live out the law. Our security is the grace of God. The grace of God is our rope. This is the heart of the gospel. This is the remedy to the anxiety characteristic of old-fashioned Adventist legalism.

But to tell the whole story, I must make an additional point. Some have imagined that grace eliminates the need to climb. We rest in God. We sit on the bench and watch the climbers. There is no effort, no struggle, no creative energy expected from us. But this misses the point. God gives us grace so that we can climb. My wife sat on the bench and watched. She did not attempt the climb because at the time she was great with child. And because she was not climbing, she was not offered the rope. The only people offered the rope that afternoon were those who were climbing the wall.

God offers His grace only to those who embrace the call to holiness. God offers His grace to those who seek to be imitators of God as His dearly loved children (Eph. 5:1). "For we are God's workmanship, created in Christ Jesus to do good works" (Eph. 2:10, NIV).

Obedience is not optional. God expects us to shape our lives according to the wisdom He has given us in the law. But our eternal security is not based on our skill or achievement in ordering our lives. Our quality of life and our effectiveness in service will be strongly affected by our obedience to the law. Our eternal safety is secured by allowing God to wrap us with His grace and secure us to the Tree of Heaven. He only does this when we approach the wall and attempt the climb. But when we offer ourselves for the climb, our security, safety, and future are utterly in the hands of our heavenly Instructor. And He has never dropped a climber.

Escaping the Tyranny of Law

You will show me the path that leads to life; your presence
fills me with joy and brings me pleasure forever (Ps.16:11, TEV).

As I entered my teen years I occasionally tried my hand at cooking. I began with really complicated things such as oatmeal. I'd carefully read the directions on the oatmeal box, then just as carefully measure the ingredients into the kettle, adding them in just the order listed.

Other mornings, I watched Mother make oatmeal. She didn't measure anything. She held the kettle under the faucet for a moment or two, then added salt by pouring it into her hand before dumping it in. Once the water was boiling, she picked up the round Quaker Oatmeal box and poured. She stirred the oats a couple of times, sometimes added a bit more oats, put the lid on, and a little later served breakfast.

She had much the same approach to biscuits. Dump in some flour. Dump in some sugar. Pour a bit of salt into her hand and dump that in. She did use a spoon for the baking powder, but did not use a measuring cup for the milk or oil.

Now, when I made biscuits, I got out the cookbook and read the directions a dozen times. I used a knife to level off each cup of flour as I measured it. I used measuring spoons for salt and sugar and baking powder. I used a glass measuring cup for the milk and oil. Then I carefully counted the number of times I turned the dough. (Betty Crocker says to knead it 15 times.)

As a teenager in Memphis and later as a bachelor in my own apartment in Times Square, I dreamed of escaping the tyranny of the cookbook. I wished I could dump and stir like Mother. So I tried. And I threw away pots of oatmeal too salty to eat and trays of biscuits that even the dog couldn't chew. So it was back to the recipes.

But over time, amazingly, it has happened. I can now cook oatmeal without reading the directions on the side of the box, and my kids will eat it (most of the time). I can make pretty good biscuits without pulling down the cookbook. I even serve them to company.

I've been delivered from the tyranny of recipes.

Which is a silly thing to say. If you cook at all, you know what's really happened—the law of teaspoons and cups has moved from the side of the oatmeal box into my head and hands. Whether I use a teaspoon or my hand to measure the salt, whether I use a measuring cup or estimate as I pour the oats from the box, edible oatmeal results from getting the proportions right.

It is certainly more convenient to have the proportions in my mind than to be a slave to the words and numbers on the side of the box. I prefer dumping and stirring to measuring. And having internalized the proportions, I'm free to innovate. I can add raisins to the oatmeal or apple slices and dates. I can make sweet biscuits for strawberry shortcake. But the only way to make good oatmeal or delicious biscuits is to approximate the proportions printed on the box or in the book.

So with life. The only way to build a good life is to approximate the laws written in the Book. Sure, slavish attention to the details of the law is not the mark of a mature Christian. And the law works better as internalized principles than as a collection of specific rules. But those who think they can make a better life by escaping the tyranny of the law will probably end up with oatmeal that's as salty as Fritos and biscuits as hard as rocks.

God Is Watching

The Lord said to Samuel, "Do not be impressed that he is handsome or tall because I have rejected him. The Lord does not see as man sees. People judge by appearances, but the Lord sees the heart" (see 1 Sam. 16:7).

But the thing David had done displeased the Lord (2 Sam.11:27, NIV).

You may remember my mentioning Milton in the introduction to this book. He had been attending the Church of the Advent Hope for just a few weeks when he asked to join. He had grown up Adventist in Kingston, Jamaica, had left the church in his late teens, and now in his 60s was wanting to reconnect with his spiritual home. But I put him off. Something didn't seem right. Besides, he gave me an excuse to put him off. In that congregation, the way you "joined" was by becoming a member of a Sabbath school class. After you had participated in a class for two months the class would recommend you to the church for acceptance into membership. Milton did not attend Sabbath school; he couldn't get up that early.

He and I met on Tuesdays to study the Bible and converse about spiritual life. He was impatient with the delay, but he seemed to enjoy our times together. He regularly scolded me for not running our church the way an Adventist church was supposed to be run—we didn't start Sabbath school with a song service at 9:15, there was no secretary's report or mission reading during Sabbath school. In other words, we didn't do things the way he remembered them from his childhood. But he kept attending church and keeping his appointments with me.

After a couple months he cautiously began to reveal the horrible secret that explained much of the bitterness I had sensed. Shortly after he had moved to the States, his sister and her husband had also left Jamaica and settled in Westchester County just north of New York City. They joined the local Adventist church. Their children grew up attending the local Adventist church. In their teen years they asked to be baptized. The pastor refused. He insisted his church was for White people. There were other churches for Black people, and Milton's nephews and nieces could go there to be baptized. These young people got the message of rejection loudly and clearly. They all left the church. Several became involved with drugs. Some went to jail. All of them had marriage problems. And Milton traced all of this heartbreak back to their humiliating rejection in that suburban church.

Milton had no children of his own. These nieces and nephews were his surrogate children. The brokenness of their lives tore his heart. For decades he had nursed an understandable but soul-bending resentment against that pastor. Every time Milton heard about another difficulty in the lives of his nieces and nephews his hatred was given fresh fire.

Now Milton was trying to reconnect with God. He wanted to reconnect with the church of his childhood, but as we talked it became clear that he could never experience any kind of healthy connection with either the church or God unless he let go of his resentment and bitterness. But how could he? How could he forgive the monstrous evil done by that minister? If he let go of his anger, wasn't that tacitly condoning or at least excusing what the minister had done to his nieces and nephews? Besides, how could he trust God to deal with the situation inasmuch as the evil had been done by one of His own ministers?

We talked about the judgment. We looked at Jesus' words about the judgment as seeing through religious profession and even religious miracle-working to the actual behavior and character of people (Matt. 7:13-27). We read the stern words of warning about the doom awaiting those who damage children (Matt. 18:6-9). Slowly Milton found release. He found it was safe to release the wicked minister to the judgment of God because God was not going to be fooled by the man's title or spirituality.

Eventually Milton was baptized and joined the church. He never did get used to the fact that we didn't do Sabbath school "right," but he frequently told newcomers that this church and this crazy pastor had saved his life. He was set free. And one of the key tools in that deliverance was the biblical picture of judgment.

In the Old Testament, judgment is often pictured as good news. Note the glee, the ecstasy, inspired by the prospect of judgment in these passages from Psalms: "Tell the nations, 'The Lord is King.' The earth is set, and it cannot be moved. He will judge the people fairly. Let the skies rejoice and the earth be glad; let the sea and everything in them shout. Let the fields and everything in them rejoice. Then all the trees of the forest will sing for joy before the Lord, because he is coming. He is coming to judge the world; he will judge the world with fairness and the peoples with truth" (Ps. 96:10-13, NCV).

"Shout for joy to the Lord, all the earth, burst into jubilant song with music; make music to the Lord with the harp, with the harp and the sound of singing, with trumpets and the blast of the ram's horn—shout for joy before the Lord, the King. Let the sea resound, and everything in it, the world, and all who live in it. Let the rivers clap their hands, let the mountains sing together for joy; let them sing before the Lord, for he comes to judge the earth. He will judge the world in righteousness and the people with equity (Ps. 98:4-9, NIV).

Why this eager anticipation of judgment? Because judgment is the time of the grand reversal. The powerless—the poor, the fatherless, the widow, and the world of nature—will finally be delivered from the tyranny of the powerful and willful. The Bible is filled with anticipation for the day when God will knock the high and mighty off their lofty perches and raise up the downtrodden. And judgment is the inauguration of that new day. "He has done mighty deeds by his power. He has scattered the people who are proud and think great things about themselves. He has brought down rulers from their thrones and raised up the humble. He has filled the hungry with good things and sent the rich away with nothing" (Luke 1:51-53, NCV).

These reversals are the fruit of judgment. In the Old Testament, it is the poor and powerless who plead for judgment to come. Their sole confidence is in God's justice and strength. "Happy is he who has the God of Jacob for his help, whose hope is in the Lord his God, . . . who executes justice for the oppressed, who gives food to the hungry. The Lord sets free the prisoners" (Ps.146:5-7, Amplified).

In a psalm written for King Solomon but with clear messianic overtones we read: "He will judge Your people with righteousness, and Your poor with justice. . . . He will save the children of the needy, and will break in pieces the oppressor" (Ps. 72:2-4, NKJV).

When we read "poor" we could just as well read "powerless." In this world, the powerful get what they want, the rest get what they can. Why is it that in the United States, the death penalty is imposed almost exclusively on convicts who are poor, black, or brown? Are they the only heinous killers? No. They have the least power.

While poor people in the United States probably have more opportunities and rights than poor people at any other time or place in human history, the fact remains that the poor suffer disproportionately the severest penalties of the law. They have less influence in government. They have fewer options for the education of their children. They can more readily be victimized by people with greater financial resources.

But God is watching. Judgment day is coming. Then God will restore the moral balance. "For the Lord your God is God of gods and Lord of lords, the great God, mighty and awesome, who shows no partiality nor takes a bribe. He executes ("judgment of," KJV; "administers justice for," NKJV; "defends the cause of," NIV; "defends the rights of," CEV) the fatherless and the widow, and loves the stranger, giving him food and clothing" (see Deut. 10:17, 18).

"Lord, You have heard the desire of the humble. You will prepare their heart. You will cause your ear to hear. To judge the fatherless and the oppressed, that the man of the earth may oppress no more" (Ps.10:17-19).

"Behold my servant, whom I uphold; mine elect, in whom my soul delighteth; I have put my spirit upon him: he shall bring forth judgment to the Gentiles. He shall not cry, nor lift up, nor cause his voice to be heard in the street. A bruised reed shall he not break, and the smoking flax shall he not quench: he shall bring forth judgment unto truth. He shall not fail nor be discouraged, till he have set judgment in the earth: and the isles shall wait for his law" (Isa. 42:1-4, KJV).

This passage highlights the implacable resolve of the Messiah to address the problems of injustice. When the Messiah comes, He will not just smooth everything over. He will not smilingly give a pass to those who affect a religious posture but are heavy-handed in their dealings with those who have less power.

In this life, justice is vanishingly rare. If there is no future balancing of the moral accounts, then justice is at best illusory. Without a future judgment to redress the reality of injustice in this world, the very concept of justice becomes a cruel joke. And Karl Marx would be vindicated in referring to religion as the opiate of the masses. It offers to numb our sense of outrage but does nothing to fix the problems. The doctrine of judgment provides a stern reality check on the popular Christian notion that religion is simply an affirmation of the essential goodness of all people and of their blessed future..

Not only is God watching; God will act.

This picture of judgment allowed Milton to release his resentment. He understood that his forgiving the minister did not excuse the minister. It simply released Milton himself from the ball and chain of negativity and bitterness. What had been done to his family was damnable evil, and God was watching. God holds Himself responsible for addressing the violence done to the powerless. That wasn't Milton's job. When Milton let go of his anger he could count on God to remember, to avenge, to somehow balance the moral scales of the universe. And God would do a far better job than Milton ever could.

The doctrine of judgment provides the stern reality that undergirds the Bible's call for us to exercise the gentleness of forgiveness. When we forgive we release our claim against the evildoer. We surrender our right to reparations for the damage done to us. Often, forgiveness feels like giving a pass to the person who has harmed us. It feels like we are somehow saying that what they have done is not all that bad, that it is understandable or excusable. In reality, when forgiveness is properly coupled with the doctrine of judgment, it is a declaration that what was done was damnable.

If what the person did to us was not all that bad, we would excuse them. Forgiveness is not excusing. Forgiveness means labeling what was done as thoroughgoing wickedness. It cannot be excused or explained away or laughed off. So we forgive; that is, we release our obsession with the evil and the evildoer. We release them to God's judgment, knowing that He is far more capable of bringing them to justice than we are.

This picture of the role of judgment can serve as a powerful help to those who have been abused by clergy, fathers who were leaders in the church, or mothers who were celebrated for their religious service. The doctrine of judgment insists that God is watching.

God is watching, and He cannot be fooled—even by great religiosity. One of the most popular figures in the history of ancient Israel was David who as a lad had defeated the giant, Goliath, and eventually became king. After he had been king for a long time, he had an affair with the wife of Uriah, one of his military officers who was away on an extended military campaign. When the woman became pregnant, David recalled Uriah from the front, hoping to make it appear the child was actually his. When that failed, David arranged for Uriah to be killed in battle in such a way as to appear accidental. After a discrete period of mourning, David took Bathsheba into the palace as his wife.

At this point in the story the Bible inserts a simple but dramatic sentence: "But the thing David had done displeased the Lord" (2 Sam. 11:27, NIV). It is important to understand David's status in the Bible. He is presented as a special friend of God. God uses David's spiritual devotion and religious zeal as a standard against which He compares all the subsequent kings of Israel. David is referred to throughout the Bible as a model or symbol of the Messiah, the great future King who will bring about the ultimate triumph of God on earth. But all of this status did nothing to blind God. When David violated another person, God was not pleased. David experienced severe punishment because God was watching.

And God still watches. That is the meaning of judgment. If denominational leaders transfer a minister or teacher who has a known pattern of damaging parishioners or students, God is watching. If a congregation fails to act in disciplining a member who is a pedophile, God is watching. If a powerful political figure harasses women, God is watching. If a devout woman makes a habit of repeating what she knows about the frailties of others (gossip), God is watching. If a boss is a jerk, if an employee is a flake, if a prosecutor or lawyer is dishonest, God is watching. And He will act.

It is vital to remember that in His watching, God is not fooled by religious and social status. He examines the totality of a person. He looks clear through the persona that people project at church or to the media or to their communities. He watches what happens at home when there is no company to impress, what happens in the conference room when no regulators are present. God is not impressed with religious credentials. Abusive church folk, belligerent or dishonest clergy, "spiritual" philanderers, all will discover in the judgment that their religious postures simply earn them greater condemnation. Victims will be delighted to learn that God could not be bought, bullied, bamboozled, flummoxed, intimidated, snookered, or influenced.

God will judge on the basis of reality. He will balance the scales of justice. He will see justice done. Victims can trust Him. Oppressors beware.

God is watching.

Good People but Unbelievers

There will be weeping and grinding of teeth when you see Abraham, Isaac, Jacob, and all the prophets in the kingdom of God, but you yourselves thrown outside. People will come from east and west and north and south and take their places at the feast in the kingdom of God. Indeed there are those who are last who will be first, and first who will be last (see Luke 13:28-30).

Historically, Adventists have linked their concern for the importance and authority of the law with another concept we call the investigative judgment. The idea of God closely investigating everything one has ever thought or done is pretty scary. But as we have continued to study the Bible's teaching about judgment, we have found that judgment is not just a scary reminder that God is watching when we are pursuing mischief. It is also a strong statement about the justice of God. It assures us that ultimate salvation is not based on arbitrary decisions by God or the "luck" of being born in the right place at the right time.

Janet's heart was utterly broken. While her son, Billy, was alive, she had prayed and hoped. But how do you live with no hope? He had died several weeks before in an auto accident. The ache of losing him in this life was unbearable. But since he wasn't a believer, she knew she would never see him again. Ever. "He left the church when he was a teenager," she told me, "and made no pretense of being a Christian. And the accident was so sudden. He never had a chance."

Billy had been speeding through the Santa Monica Mountains in his Mazda Miata. He missed a turn and hit a massive live oak just feet from the pavement. No time for a last minute conversion.

At the funeral people said all kinds of nice things. When someone needed help, Billy was there. When someone was in jail and needed a friend to come and pick them up, who did they call? Billy. When someone broke up with a girlfriend and had to move out of their apartment on short notice, whose couch did he land on? Billy's. When Billy's dad had an accident that put him in bed for six months, who took off work and waited on him hand and foot? And who kept his mom's swimming pool immaculately clean and her lawn manicured after her husband dumped her to chase a shorter skirt? Billy. I figured all this was just funeral talk, the nice things people feel obliged to say in the face of the darkness of death. But in talking with people after the funeral, I heard repeated private validation of the public statements.

I recounted some of this to Janet, then asked, "Was Billy really like that?"

"Yes, he was."

"Then you can hope to see him again."

"How? How can you say I can see him again when he was so far away from God?"

"What do you mean, 'when he was so far away from God'?"

"Well, the fact that he left the church and wasn't a Christian and didn't believe in God, as far as I know, and had no use for the church or religion."

The Bible celebrates faith. It even declares that without faith it is impossible to please God (Heb. 11:6). But it also teaches that God is able to make very sophisticated judgments about faith.

The Bible explicitly states that if a person talks like an angel but acts like a devil, his actions mean more than his words (Matt. 7; James 2). The opposite can also be true. People may deny with their words a faith that is evident in their lives.

This is illustrated in the ministry of Jesus. Once, a Roman officer came asking for help for a favorite servant who was at home, sick. The officer told Jesus, You don't need to come. "Just say the word, and my servant will be healed" (Matt. 8:8, NIV). Even though this man was not Jewish, Jesus declared his faith superior to anything He had seen among the people of God. On other occasions, Jesus encountered people who were possessed by demons. In every case, these folks expressed their faith by shouting at Jesus and protesting His approach to torture them. Jesus ignored their words and responded to some unspoken cry of their heart and saved them from the demons.

In the judgment, God will be able to read the hearts of many who left the church (or never were part of it) and see the real faith hidden in their lives. Their words may be no more expressive of faith than were the protestations of the people who were possessed by demons, but God will read the faith expressed in their deeds of mercy.

Often those who say they reject God are actually rejecting a caricature of God—a caricature that we, too, reject. In Billy's case, it was easy to make sense of his actions. His dad had made a great show of religion, then dumped Billy's mom for someone else. During Billy's teen years, the pastor and the youth leader at his church became involved in scandalous affairs. Then the Bible teacher at the parochial high school he attended went off the deep end theologically and, finally, psychologically. Almost every man Billy knew who should have served as a model of God violated Billy's trust. When Billy turned his back on God and the church, he wasn't rejecting the true God who is faithful and compassionate. He was rejecting pretense, hypocrisy, and dishonesty. He refused to believe in a God who would condone injustice and faithlessness.

In the crucifixion of Christ, God demonstrated the strength of His intention to save people (Rom. 5:8). Though no one can pay his or her own moral indebtedness and live, through the crucifixion Jesus paid the moral debt of every human (1 John 2:2). So it would be appropriate to ask why would anyone be excluded from heaven. The judgment is the public, visible process of determining who will fit into the society of heaven, who will enjoy a culture of service. Many who call themselves nonbelievers will discover, when all the misunderstandings have been swept away, that God is precisely the ideal to whom they devoted their lives.

The most famous picture of the judgment in the Bible is a story Jesus told. He pictures God as a shepherd separating his sheep and goats. The sheep are the good people and the goats are the bad people. The sheep are commended for their goodness, which consisted of giving God food when He was hungry, water when He was thirsty and visits when He was incarcerated. The sheep protest they never saw God hungry, thirsty, or incarcerated. God responds, "What you did to the lowliest persons, you did to me" (Matt. 25:40). The goats are excluded because they refused to give care. The great divide between the saved and the lost is in how they responded to down-to-earth human need, not how spiritual were their words.

The story of the sheep and the goats does not contradict the theory that we are saved by faith, but it does qualify it. In reality, neither faith nor works is the fundamental cause of our salvation; rather, we are saved by grace—the generous, merciful activity of God. "Faith" and "works" are different ways of describing the human yielding to grace. God has given us a number of ways to express our faith: baptism, the Lord's Supper, Sabbathkeeping, and, of course, words. But trumping all of these is the gift of opportunities to serve.

Ultimately God is judge. But because of Jesus' words about the sheep and the goats, I could offer strong hope to Janet about Billy. We are confident that many who are not Christians will be saved at last. They'll be in heaven because God will read their hearts and see that what they rejected was not Him but a false god. God will demonstrate to the universe that through their care for people in need these unbelievers were, in fact, serving Jesus in camouflage. Their real loyalty is to the values of heaven. They have not earned heaven by their good deeds, but they have demonstrated a wordless faith in the God who saves. And God will take great delight in astonishing them with His invitation, "Come, you who are blessed by my Father; take your inheritance, the kingdom prepared for you since the creation of the world" (Matt. 25:34, NIV).

A Thousand Years of Answers

*Judge nothing before the designated time. Wait until the Lord comes.
He will bring to light what is hidden in darkness and will expose the
motives of men's hearts (see 1 Cor. 4:5).*

*Do not be afraid. There is nothing concealed that will not be unveiled
or hidden that will not be revealed (see Matt. 10:26).*

Adventists have specialized in the biblical prophecies about the end of
time. When we tell the story of the last days we begin with the investigative judgment mentioned in the previous chapter. Throughout the
Bible the judgment is always pictured as a very public event. God does not
make the decisions about an individual's destiny in the privacy of His own
mind but in the presence of countless witnesses, heavenly beings who provide an independent verification that the decisions are based on reality and
not a carefully edited version of the person's life.

This court process begins in heaven before Jesus returns to earth,
while life here continues its normal course. When the judgment is finished, Jesus returns to earth. (This is the Second Coming.) The dazzling
brilliance of the unveiled presence of divinity annihilates the wicked, but
announces rescue to the godly. Jesus resurrects the righteous dead, then
transports them together with the godly who are still alive to a glorious
paradise called heaven, where they live and reign with Christ for a thousand years—the famous millennium of Revelation 20. Apparently, the
only life here on earth during the millennium is the devil and his
demons.

At the end of the millennium, the residence of the godly, the New
Jerusalem, is returned to earth, and the wicked are raised to life again.
The devil and his demons busy themselves rallying the wicked for a final
desperate attempt to establish dominance by capturing the New
Jerusalem.

As the hordes of the wicked assemble to attack the Holy City, they
are interrupted by the appearance in the sky of a great white throne with
Jesus seated on it. All the wicked are arraigned before the throne. They
are confronted with the irrefutable evidence of the justice of their condemnation. Crushed by the vivid picture of their folly and evil, they re-

luctantly bow and acknowledge that God is right. They do not worship. They do not yield their hearts. But they grudgingly admit the truth: God is right; they are wrong. Even the devil bows and angrily acknowledges that God is right.

Having bowed, however, the devil summons some last bit of rebellious courage. He calls for his followers to join him in an assault on the city, and some rise to join him. But the entire judgment process has reached its conclusion, and fire descends from heaven to purify the earth in preparation for the re-creation of a perfect biosphere. The wicked, including the devil himself, die in this conflagration.

From that point forward begins the fulfillment of the promise: Now the dwelling of God is with people. He will live with them. They will be His people; He will live with them and be their God. He will wipe every tear from their eyes. There will be no more death or mourning or crying or pain, for the old order has passed away (see Rev. 21:3, 4).

So What Does This Story Mean?

We might not have every detail in our story correct. But the point of the story is what it says about the character of God. We must connect our theories about the events at the end of human history with the picture of God given in the ministry and death of Jesus. The moral of the story, even the scary stories in Revelation, is, God is love. On one hand, if the story did not include any scary elements, we would dismiss it as utterly disconnected from the real world we live in. On the other hand, if the story does not help us transcend the fear and anxiety of this world, why bother telling it?

Hell

Conventional Christian thinking for much of the last 2,000 years has seen hell as a place of eternal burning. This doctrine was rooted in the Greek philosophical notion of the soul as inherently immortal. The body was ephemeral; the soul was the real essence of a person, and it was absolutely indestructible. So if the soul did not go to heaven, it had to go somewhere else. That somewhere else was hell, a place of endless flames. Later the notion of purgatory was added to offer hope for people who appeared to be too good for hell but not good enough for heaven.

Adventists disagree with this common understanding on three grounds. First, only God is intrinsically immortal (1 Tim. 1:17). Eternal life is available to humans only as a supernatural gift (John 3:16). We do not believe there is a naturally immortal soul available for the torments of an ever-burning hell. We believe a person is an indivisible whole (Gen. 2:7).

If the physical body dies, that means the whole person is dead. There is no separate soul that can inhabit a place called "hell."

Second, the Bible's statements about hell are better interpreted as referring to an event rather than a place. These "fires of hell" happen at the end of time and are designed to purify the earth in preparation for its re-creation. These fires are unstoppable in intensity but definitely limited in time (Matt. 13:36-43).

Third, it is inconceivable that a loving God would sustain souls for billions of years for the sole purpose of torturing them. The prophet Ezekiel wrote that God takes no pleasure in the death of the wicked (Eze. 33:11). Jesus said that it is God's "good pleasure" to give the kingdom to His disciples. The crucifixion of Jesus is a stunning demonstration that God would actually rather die than live without us. In light of this, the notion of eternal torment is simply unimaginable.

Who Will Be Lost?

Given the facts that Jesus died for the sins "of the whole world" (1 John 2:2) and that God does not wish anyone to perish (2 Peter 3:9), why would anyone be excluded from heaven? The answer is not simple, but one classic response of Adventism is that those who are lost would find heaven a place of torment.

The Bible paints vivid pictures of the society God has in mind. "They shall not hurt or destroy in all my holy mountain" (Isa.11:9, AB). "There will be no more death or mourning or crying or pain, for the old order of things has passed away" (Rev. 21:5). "In keeping with his promise we are looking forward to a new heaven and a new earth where righteousness will be at home" (2 Peter 3:13). For some people such an environment would be torture. Imagine Hitler assigned an apartment next door to a rabbi, or Stalin being required to yield his will to the directions of a kulak superior, or a member of the KKK being asked to sit next to an African-American at a heavenly feast.

If, at the last minute, God offered the wicked a passport to heaven, any who accepted the offer would find heaven a miserable place. Heaven would be unending torment to those who have defined themselves through selfishness, oppression, and narcissism. We shape our futures through our present choices.

The great challenge for God is to win our hearts, to persuade us to open our lives to the shaping of the Holy Spirit. If we resist the values of heaven here, we would find them oppressive there.

In Revelation 20 we see that when the wicked are raised to life they immediately join a movement to attack the city. They do not change their minds. They do not plead for inclusion in the peaceful society. They are stubbornly, adamantly rebellious. This story offers a visual confirmation of the judgment of heaven. If people were given a second chance, they would make the same choice they did the first time.

Answers to My Questions

One of the most persistent obstacles to faith is the problem of suffering. How can a good, powerful God allow the misery of this world to continue so long? Most of the useful answers to the questions surrounding suffering have to do with the nature of freedom and love. But while these explanations offer hints of rationality in the sea of human hurt, they never reach the bottom of our heartwrenching angst. They don't answer the questions, Why my daughter? Why my son? Or my lover, my friend, myself?

Some religious systems dismiss the questions. God is God, you are a mere human. You should submit to God and quit asking silly questions. But they are not silly questions. They are huge questions. And they go to the heart of the questions, Is God good? Is God trustworthy? Why should I worship?

The story of the millennium helps us deal with these questions. Revelation 20:4 states that during the thousand years the redeemed will act as judges. What does this mean? The eternal fate of every human being has already been decided. God doesn't need assistance in figuring out the hard cases. The most likely subject of these judges is God Himself. In the investigative judgment, the lives of people are examined to determine their eternal destiny. In the millennial judgment, the records of heaven are examined to build our confidence in God.

The saved will have a thousand years to investigate to their own satisfaction whether God's actions have been more than fair. The saints will be able to trace all the lines of evidence that support God's decisions. This thousand-year opportunity demonstrates how much God respects your questions. In this life, God says Trust Me. In that life, God will say Test Me. Now we live by faith. Then we will live by sight.

The investigative judgment lays the foundation for the millennial judgment by creating a publicly attested record of God and humanity. The records available for scrutiny during the millennium are not video tapes that God pulls out of His pocket or His personal archives. Obviously, God could create whatever impression He wanted by editing the records. Richard Nixon erased audio tapes. NBC TV faked a safety test on Chevrolet trucks. If God wanted to, He, too, could doctor the record and we'd never know.

The investigative judgment doesn't happen inside God's mind. This is why it takes time. It is a public process conducted in the presence of tens of thousands, perhaps thousands of millions of angels. When each case is presented and decided, the angels sign off on the record. They observed what happened. They can testify whether or not God's version of the events is accurate. And, of course, it is.

So when the judgment is over and Jesus has gathered His people from earth and taken them to heaven, the record available for our examination is one that was created in an open court. This is our guarantee of an accurate record.

That's how much God respects our questions. That's how far He will go to win our confidence. God loves us and wants us to trust Him. He is willing to do anything lawful to win our love and affection. He'll even give us a thousand years to process our questions and to recover from the grief and heartbreak characteristic of this world.

If you are a believer with a simple confidence in God and have no questions, I'm sure there will be other things to do in heaven besides poring over ancient records. But if your spiritual life is characterized by questioning and perplexity, the millennial judgment pictures a time of final resolution. We will finally find rest from our questions. We will receive a full accounting of divine activity (and inactivity). God loves us so much that He will not get on with the business of eternity until He has responded to every human question. That's how much He respects us. That's how much He cares.

After the Millennium

The Adventist version of the story of the universe begins with a loving God creating beings in His own image who could respond to His love and participate in a joyous, creative friendship. We then follow the story into the dark, heartbreaking world warped and bruised by evil, the world we live in. A world haunted with unanswered and unanswerable questions about justice and love, human freedom and divine initiative, foreknowledge and responsibility. We ache with a desperate hunger to understand how a loving God can tolerate a world that has become intolerable to us.

But the story moves forward. It ends with the restoration of unalloyed love. Every human question has been answered, every doubt has been addressed. Questioners have come to confident, joyous trust. But humans are not the only ones pictured as enjoying a new level of trust. God Himself demonstrates an amazing trust in humans by giving them a Godlike status in the universe. God is still God, humans are still human, but we have become so close that God and humans are pictured sharing power and work. Jesus announces, "To the one who overcomes, I will offer a place on my throne, even as I overcame and am sitting on my Father's throne" (Rev. 3:21). This picture of divine power-sharing is the ultimate declaration that truly God is love.